FORCED MARCH FROM THE BULGE TO BERCHTESGADEN

By John J. Mohn

Copyright 2024
Published Massillon, Ohio 2024

Memoir by Major John J. Mohn
Foreword by Edward P. McHugh
Introduction by Mandy Altimus Stahl
Biography by Debora Mohn Altimus
Book prepared by Richard Altimus
Edited by Richard Altimus, Debora Mohn Altimus, and Mandy Altimus Stahl

Printed in the United States of America
ISBN: 978-0-9863465-4-5
Second Printing

On the cover:
American soldiers of the 75th Division march along the snow covered road on the way to cut off the St. Vith-Houffalize road in Belgium January 24, 1945
Image courtesy National Archives

Cover design by Mandy Altimus Stahl

DEDICATION

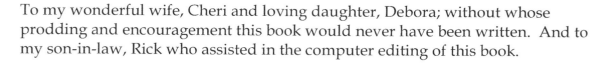

To my wonderful wife, Cheri and loving daughter, Debora; without whose prodding and encouragement this book would never have been written. And to my son-in-law, Rick who assisted in the computer editing of this book.

Editor's Note: Additional thanks to granddaughter, Mandy Altimus Stahl, who helped with the publishing of her Grandpa's book.

CHAPTER OUTLINE

Contents

FOREWORD

When World War II's Battle of the Bulge began with a surprise German attack on the 16th of December, 1944, troops of the U.S. Army's 106th Infantry Division occupied the most exposed American positions. They had been on the European continent for less than two weeks, and cut off from reinforcements, were left to face the German onslaught alone. They fought back, but as their ammunition, food and medical supplies dwindled and the enemy noose drew tighter, over 7,000 were ordered by their commanding officers to surrender to the surrounding German forces. Except for the Bataan Death March this was the largest surrender of American troops in World War II.

Major John Mohn of Akron, Ohio, the author of this book, was the Operations Officer of the Division's 1st Battalion, 422nd Infantry Regiment. He was a citizen soldier, who had volunteered to join the Army as a private in 1941. This is the story of his 1,200 mile odyssey as a prisoner of war (POW) to the far reaches of the Nazi empire during which he and his fellow soldiers were starved, frozen, bombed, and shot at.

Because the German military was unprepared to absorb a massive influx of American prisoners and had little space to house them, Major Mohn's imprisonment became an almost continuous five month march through a collapsing and chaotic Third Reich. Initially he was sent to a camp for American officers over 500 miles away in Poland. He arrived there only to be marched out of the camp a few days later when Russian forces broke through the German lines around Warsaw. Seeing the prisoners as a potential bargaining chip and intent on keeping them out of Russian hands, the Germans forced the Americans to make a harrowing march westward across rural Poland and Germany in the dead of winter just ahead of pursuing Soviet forces. After this month and a half ordeal, the prisoners finally arrived at the Hammelburg POW Camp in northern Bavaria, only about 100 miles away from where they started. Two weeks later this camp was attacked and briefly captured by a task force of General Patton's Third Army. The Germans, however, soon recaptured the camp and immediately sent Major Mohn and the other prisoners on another dangerous march which ended at the Austrian border five weeks later when they were liberated by American troops. Through it all, Major Mohn persevered and returned to the United States where he underwent treatment and rehabilitation for the injuries he had suffered as a POW. He returned to civilian life and developed a highly successful career as a

Foreword by Edward P. McHugh

psychologist. But his remarkable experiences in the military never quite left him. Eventually he put words to paper and the result is the book you have before you – one of very few accounts of this type ever to have been published. More than just a narrative of his experiences as a POW, it is a testament to the indomitable spirit of American soldiers and a reminder to all of us of the sacrifices they made to preserve our freedom.

- Edward P. McHugh

INTRODUCTION: BEFORE THE BULGE

By Mandy Altimus Stahl

John J. Mohn while at Akron University, Fraternity Phi Kappa Tau, 1940
Debora Mohn Altimus personal collection.

About 1937, while attending Akron University, John Mohn took ROTC (Reserve Officers' Training Corps). John had no desire to become an officer, but by the end of this training, he had reached the rank of 2nd Lieutenant.

In preparation of what appeared to be inevitable world conflict, Congress passed the Selective Service Act of 1940. This was the first peacetime conscription in U.S. history. Enacted in September 1940, this act required men between 21 and 35 years of age to register with local draft boards. Men were drafted by a lottery system, and were required to serve for twelve months. After that year was completed, John was told he would be draft-free and not required to sign up, should a war arise. On February 4, 1941, John decided to enlist for this program, and join the Navy. He drove to Cleveland, entered the Armory, and began the process. He took the written test, passed the physical, and was about to be sworn in when the commanding officer at the Armory said that John's teeth protruded too much and they would not accept him. John stated in an interview that "this is stupid" and went to the other end of the Armory and enlisted in the Army. At this moment he could have enlisted as a 2nd Lieutenant because of his ROTC training. It apparently slipped his mind and he enlisted as a Private.

John Mohn at Camp Clairbourne, Louisiana, 1941.
Debora Mohn Altimus personal collection.

John was assigned to the 37th Division at Camp Shelby, Mississippi. He volunteered for the Signal Company on teletype. The day after he signed up, the teletype was discontinued, so he was reassigned to supply in the Signal Company.

First row: Cpl. J. J. Mohn, J. W. Cope, E. F. Poland, P.F.C. P. Jones, P.F.C. E. Sherman, L. S. Hunt, Stf. Sgt. G. H. Martin, 1st Sgt. S. E. Morris. *Second row:* P.F.C. B. C. Morse, P.F.C. P. K. White, P.F.C. W. O. Hershberger, R. H. Berry, W. G. Lineback, P. E. Tomlinson, H. Skurow, Sgt. E. J. Weger, D. E. Berger, A. Maxim. *Third row:* P.F.C. H. P. Mallon, W. R. King, Sgt. J. P. Irwin, C. A. Starks, R. B. Hunter, P.F.C. E. E. Tomlinson, P.F.C. G. W. Kenne, W. C. Allen, R. C. Muelheim, E. L. Hagedorn, R. A. Osborn. *Fourth row:* P.F.C. W. A. Brooks, E. R. Robinson, P.F.C. O. R. Gilbert, F. A. Herbst, J. F. Schuett, P.F.C. K. S. Garinger, M. D. Cassidy, J. M. Downey, P.F.C. C. J. Marx, Cpl. M. F. Olshawsky, Sgt. H. C. Clawson, Stf. Sgt. R. M. Bunnell.

John Mohn in the 37ᵗʰ Division yearbook, 1943.

He was sent to Indiantown Gap near Carlisle, Pennsylvania. During his time at camp his mother, Birdie Pauline Isenhour, passed away. On December 7, 1941, the Japanese attacked Pearl Harbor and the next day upon request from President Franklin Delano Roosevelt, Congress declared war on Japan and their ally Germany. This canceled the draft-free status that John had signed up for, as he had not completed his twelve months of training. His division was scheduled to board a ship headed to Japan and the Pacific Theater of the war, but the boat blew up before they could head out.

John J. Mohn and sister-in-law Helen Mohn at Indiantown Gap, Pennsylvania, 1942.
Debora Mohn Altimus personal collection.

Unidentified man, Stan Krisena (tent buddy and friend), and John J. Mohn
at Indiantown Gap, Pennsylvania, 1942.
Debora Mohn Altimus personal collection.

Aerial view of Indiantown Gap, Pennsylvania, 1942.
Debora Mohn Altimus personal collection.

John was sent to Fort Benning, Georgia, for officer training from February through April 1942. In late 1942, he was sent to Camp Forest in Telehoma, Tennessee and assigned to the 80th Division for a year. He became a company commander of the 80th Division, 319th Infantry Regiment, Company F, 1st Battalion. His division was in charge of clearing trees in the mountains in preparation for war games, to train men in firing artillery and surviving in realistic battle situations. John was in charge of the logistics and planning for the war games.

John's sister-in-law, Helen Mohn, John Mohn, and John's first wife, Katie, c.1941.
Debora Mohn Altimus personal collection.

The 80th Division was then incorporated into the 106th Division. John was reassigned as Battalion Operations Officer and sent to Camp Atterbury, Indianapolis, Indiana and assigned to the 106th Division, 422 Infantry Regiment, 1st Battalion, Headquarters Company. John reached the rank of Captain, and was told that he was the youngest Captain in the Division. As Operations Officer, he was in charge of logistics for troop movements. He staged a large 3,000-troop parade in Indianapolis in 1944.

Photograph of the parade that John Mohn planned and executed, 1944.
Debora Mohn Altimus personal collection.

In late 1944, the 106th was called up to replace the 2nd Division, weary troops stationed along the quiet Siegfried Line in the Ardennes Forest. In late October, they were loaded onto a 4-stack ship, the Aquitania, and left New York City harbor and sailed to Glasgow, Scotland. From there they were taken by truck to Fairfield, England. The troops of the 2nd Division assured the 106th Division that there would be little action on this hilly terrain in the middle of winter.

John Mohn and his brother Robert (Bus), who was in the Army Air Corps, 1945.
Altimus Family Collection.

This book is reprinted faithful to John Mohn's original memoir, completed in 2003. The family thought it best to keep his original text, as these are his memories. There may be an imprecision in town names (most of the signs were removed to confuse the enemy), or a date (not many men in the column were keeping track of the date), or some other detail. John Mohn had faithfully kept a diary during the entire march, but it was taken right after liberation. Having no record, he took down notes shortly after the war and began writing it in book form in the early 1980s. In the appendix of this book, we have reproduced two pages from Major William P. Moon's transcribed journal for reference. His journey was similar to John Mohn's.

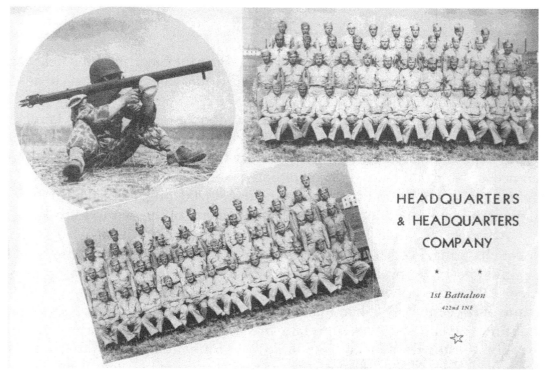

From the 106th Division Yearbook, 1944.

Detail of the page above:
John Mohn, seated, in front row, fourth from the left.

PREFACE

It was December 16, 1944, somewhere along the Siegfried Line near St. Vith, Belgium - the German counterattack that would later be referred to as the "Battle of the Bulge" had begun.

The gray, foggy dawn made a perfect umbrella for the German launching of an onslaught which nearly cost the Allies World War II. What happened at the Battle of the Bulge may be a well-known story but none of the stories make any reference to the group of American Soldiers taken prisoner at that time and marched for 140 continuous days covering over 1,200 long, cold, starvation-ridden, nightmare miles, terminated only by the end of the war in Europe.

Adversity is a mild term to describe the unbearable hardships endured by the ever changing, ever diminishing column of men. Temperatures dropped to ten degrees below zero. There were periods of fifteen days without a single bite of food. All suffered phenomenal loss of weight (I weighed sixty-five pounds by the time of liberation). We had inadequate clothing; many without hats or gloves and at times no shoes. It was especially brutal for the poor Air Corps men who were only wearing thermal boots with no soles for walking, when they were shot down and captured. The journey was marked by frozen feet, legs, arms, faces and even blood trails. Treachery, deceit and fear are just feeble attempts to put into words the anger, horror, anguish and despair felt by these military men.

The ordeal that the approximately 7,000 American Soldiers endured between December 16, 1944 and May 2, 1945, can only be epitomized by saying that a scant thirty of the original group even reached liberation as a unit. Losses of men beyond belief resulted from attempts at escape, exposure, starvation, the sadism of the German Guards and being strafed daily by our own and Allied planes.

My book is not intended as a condemnation of the German People or Army but does make reference to differing attitudes and treatment by the Wehrmacht, to whom I owe a debt of gratitude for being alive, and the Elite SS Troops, who were constantly threatening our lives with attempts to exterminate us with machine guns and failed to provide even the most basic of necessities for our daily maintenance. The German High Command seemed at a loss as to what to do with so many prisoners, and lacked a plan regarding disposition of us. The result was a wandering march covering three countries with no apparent purpose, with a final goal of holding us as hostages in Berchtesgaden at the end of the war. The consequences for us, as POWs were painfully clear. The facts and sequences of events I know first-hand because I was there from the beginning to the end. I saw dramatic changes in attitudes, values, behavior and beliefs. Hidden strengths and weaknesses in the struggle for survival were surprising and at times frightening, but the salient factor through it all was that <u>survival</u> is "All Important" and that the "Veneer of Civilization" is extremely thin.

Food line in the Ardennes Forest just before the Battle of the Bulge, 1944.
Image courtesy National Archives

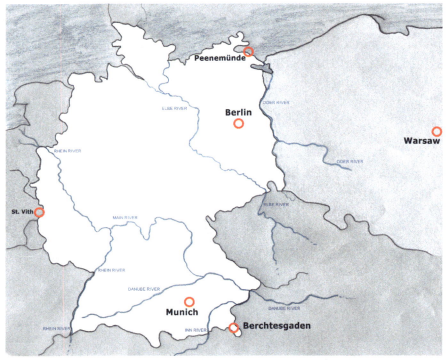

John Mohn was stationed near St. Vith, Belgium late 1944.

*Machine gunners of the 4th Armored Division covers tank crossing
snow-covered field in the Bastogne corridor, Belgium, January 3, 1945.
Image courtesy National Archives, Signal Corps (SC 364310)*

Chapter 1

THE HORROR BEGINS

I couldn't help being reminded of that famous poem by Rudyard Kipling "The Charge of the Light Brigade" on that fateful, foggy, gray, cold, drizzling morning December 16, 1944. The difference was that instead of "cannons" noted in the poem, it was tanks to the left of us, tanks to the right of us, tanks in front of us, and tanks behind us. To "charge" ahead would have been to go down the steep slope of an evergreen covered mountain. The landscape was so much like the mountain areas of Pennsylvania that it was hard to remember that we were in a foreign country fighting a very serious war. Even more serious, we were surrounded and being annihilated by German Panzer Divisions from the left and right of us. German artillery from the front was terrible enough but, to our dismay, the Germans had captured our artillery and were using our own guns to fire upon us from the rear. When we called for supporting fire, they were aiming at us instead of their own troops. Our Battalion Commander, Thomas Kent was killed by a shell coming in from the rear of our "Pill Box" command post. At first we thought our artillerymen were firing short of their target, but when we heard the German voice on our radio, we realized the awful truth - we were literally at their mercy. The divide and conquer strategy used in the German attack had been completely unexpected and totally effective. The Panzer tanks seemed as numerous as infantry men would be normally.

I was the Battalion Operations Officer for the 1st Battalion, 422nd Infantry 106th Division. We were green troops, inexperienced. We had just been brought up to strength by new and very young troops from the United States. Green and young troops refers to the fact that many of the replacements brought to us to replenish the 106th Division had come from colleges, Army Specialized Training Programs (ASTP), and other academic deferment situations. These men were about 18 years of age on the average and very angry at being called to active duty. Worse than that, their indoctrination to duty took place on cold, mud-ridden roads walking across France; along with inadequate equipment, fast movement and confusion, all of this prior to the Bulge attack. In spite of this, however, they gave a very good account of themselves in a no-win situation - where the 422nd Infantry was demolished. Army Headquarters had put us in this position, just east of St. Vith, Belgium, on the Siegfried Line, because they felt that it was the least likely place on the north south line of our front to be a point of attack - how wrong they were.

The 9th Armored Division on our left was either inundated or had pulled out, and the 28th Division on our right flank was being dissected, just as we were. After 72 hours of constant bombarding we were ordered to "attack to the rear."

Chapter 1

We had been infiltrated by English-speaking Germans and confusion was rampant. We were being systematically cut to ribbons. Elements of surviving units banded together, forming the most unlikely fighting units. There were infantry, heavy weapons, artillery, Air Corps, tank, and anti-aircraft men, all pulling together. Then, the inevitable happened - we ran out of ammunition, we were surrounded, getting point-blank fire from the German Tiger tanks and their deadly 88 millimeter guns. We were using wet, freezing ditches for cover, breaking out of traps by running behind the tanks. Many men were cut down in their tracks during these attempts. I was lucky. With 107 bullets and fragment holes in my trench coat, all the buckles shot off my boots and even my belt buckle being shot off; I was not touched by a single piece of metal. Divine Guidance or luck was to follow me through the next 5 months, through seemingly insurmountable odds. My radio operator, by my side, was not so lucky, and like so many others was killed instantly by a direct hit from an 88 millimeter tank gun.

There was something bizarre and unreal about everything happening. As I glanced over my right shoulder, I saw a Major standing dumbfounded with a spent bullet sticking rakishly out of his neck and another officer reaching over and pulling it out in a nonchalant manner, then wrapping a handkerchief around the Major's throat. My immediate and irrelevant thought was that you can't put a tourniquet around somebody's throat but I guess you can because the Major lived.

We continued to try to break out and establish a position which we could defend. As we retreated in the most orderly fashion we could, we began to accumulate men from all different units. The retreat was confused but we kept fighting with what ammunition we could find. The first night out in our retreat, we pulled into a woods for cover and to rest. Much to our amazement a large unit of German Soldiers was on the other side of this same woods. They were being as quiet as we were, not being sure, I feel, what they were facing. We could not estimate the size of this unit, and evidently they were not sure either since they made no move to come to us. Since we were out of ammunition and could not risk a confrontation, we did not move toward them, nor in anyway disclose our position. At dawn we were moving out of the woods, and noted that the Germans had already abandoned the woods during the night. We rapidly moved to the west, but we were finally completely surrounded by a solid wall of German tanks. For 2 days they circled our position, playing Benny Goodman records, shouting out over loud speakers how stupid we were to die for a lost cause and propagandizing us with the disloyalty of our wives and sweethearts at home; none of which we believed for a minute. They would then announce a five-minute break "for an artillery barrage." They continued this process until there were few trees standing in what had been a heavily-wooded, evergreen forest.

There were few men alive and not wounded. It was under these conditions that the decision to surrender was made. I will never forget the anguished cries of two young Polish soldiers who had escaped from their German captors in Poland the previous year and made their way to the United States, joining the United States Army, with the purpose of returning to the war to help liberate their own country. Now they faced with the same fate of capture once again. They pleaded with us saying, "You don't know what it is like. We have come so far and all for nothing. We will not go." Saying this, they hid in foxholes without taking into account the SS method of finally clearing an area by dropping hand grenades into all possible hiding places. We were able to pull the screaming soldiers out before they were blown to bits by grenades.

After rounding us up, the SS unit took us to a collecting point in a nearby woods and ordered immediate departure to the east. We erroneously assumed that we were to be evacuated but to our horror saw that the line was being marched past a machine gun emplacement, and men were systematically being shot down where they stood or when they passed. It was inhuman; we were outraged and scared beyond belief. No American could conceive of this kind of savagery. Some men tried to run but were shot as they left the column. Death seemed inevitable, and then again Divine Intervention in the form of a young German Wehrmacht Captain, showing as much anger and disbelief as we were showing, broke the line and shouted to us, "Don't go there, follow me, run for your lives." We needed no urging and immediately cut to our right, down a very steep mountain grade, stumbling, falling and dodging the volley of bullets from the frustrated German SS troops. It was a nightmare. We lost many men but most of us literally fell down the mountain and out of that danger.

Little did we suspect that we had just begun 140 days (almost 5 months) of constant walking, freezing, starving and living an existence that was always near death. We were headed for Koblenz and the crossing of the Rhein River into enemy territory and incarceration.

In all of our training for battle, we were never mentally prepared for the contingency of capture. The anxiety, fear, doubt and disbelief were overwhelming. The Germans had us. We were no longer free to do our own bidding. The German Captain could do with us what he chose. Stories of brutality, death, experimentation, the horrible treatment of the Jews and hundreds of other thoughts raced through our minds and chilled our blood.

"Go this way", "Go that way", "Take off your clothes", "Put your equipment here" and "Verboten", "Rausch", "Haltzen", "Kommen sie herein" all became familiar commands, always backed up with a sadistic gesture, a rifle, and a push.

Even though the Wehrmacht Captain had saved our lives, there was no love lost between us and we were quickly indoctrinated with the futility of thoughts of escape or expecting any special treatment.

Soldiers of Co. C, 48th Battalion, 7th Armored Division, garbed in snowsuits walk through the snow-covered streets of St. Vith, Belgium, January 24, 1945. Image courtesy National Archives, Signal Corps (C-682)

American P.O.W.s from the Battle of the Bulge, 1944.
Image courtesy National Archives

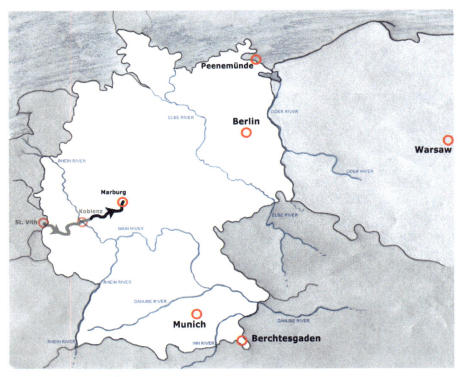

A German Tiger tank rolls past a column of American prisoners of war during the Battle of the Bulge. c.1944
Image courtesy US Military History Center

Chapter 2
THE FIRST 100 MILES WE LEARN SELF-DEFENSE

We felt lucky to be alive but we were still full of terror, dismay and confusion resulting from our recent experience. At the time we had no real idea of a destination, just relief that it wasn't a machine gun slaughter. The Captain of the German Guard was moving us along quickly and soon the sound of the intense battle began to recede. Koblenz, with its many bridges crossing the Rhein River, soon appeared downstream. We were privileged to walk along the beautiful shores of the Rhein River and see in the distance the famous "Castles on the Rhein." They soon faded from sight and memory as we encountered the confusion at the bridges which were available to cross over to Koblenz. We were all fearful and at the same time ever hopeful that our planes would bomb the bridges before we could be taken across. This seemed to us to be a very logical plan because it would stem the German reinforcements and shorten the German advance to the west and the battle field. To our dismay, there were no planes. The heavy fog and clouds had grounded all of our planes. This was one of the factors which had permitted the German Army to make the successful attack which had resulted in our being captured at this point and at this time. The darkness and overcast sky matched our spirits, and we wondered how long it would be before our planes could get into the air again and possibly save us from any further incarceration.

We started our crossing of the river; crowding, pushing, and struggling against the tide of the German soldiers being rushed to the west to reinforce their troops and their supply lines. Every type of vehicle was being employed: tanks, motorized half-tracks, horse drawn carts and even bicycles. Soldiers were walking ahead of, behind and along-side the vehicles, catching a ride when they could but always surging forward in a huge mass. It was a nightmare for everybody. Soldiers, civilians and prisoners of war all seemed to be confused.

After getting across the river, it seemed that a direction had finally been determined and I first heard of a town called Falkenberg, the only significance of this being that at that point we were supposed to be transported by train to another destination but tragically this plan was doomed to failure.

Getting out of Koblenz was no easy task. The streets we were traveling were extremely narrow, the houses being built close together and to the curbs. Koblenz was not a modern city by our standards. Masses of humanity were on the move and the German trucks and tanks were moving in the opposite direction from our column. Often it was nearly impossible to get around a tank making a turn around the corner without being crushed by it. There were angry shouts of orders from the German Guards and we did not always know what was being said but the sign language is very effective in getting a point across, especially when accompanied by a push, a shove or a rifle butt across your head. We had never really comprehended what the language barrier really meant until this time. German guttural sounds were no longer humorous but deadly serious and certainly malicious. There was a tendency on our part to silently make fun of the guttural sounds we heard. There were a few men who knew a limited number of German words which they had learned in high school or college but under these circumstances a few words didn't help much. There was a Jewish Lieutenant with us who spoke Hebrew and this was close enough to some German to suffice for communication but we did not want to make this fact known because of our knowledge of the German treatment of the Jews and we were as afraid for the Lieutenant as he was for himself.

After what seemed to be hours of pushing, shoving, dodging, cursing and running we were on our way out of Koblenz heading in a northeasterly direction which was consistent with the previously mentioned town of Falkenberg and our hopes for finally getting a ride on a train were rising.

The walking mile after mile had given us time to reflect our situation. We had settled down to some of the reality of being prisoners but I don't think anyone truly accepted it. We talked optimistically of how our Allied Forces would break through the German lines anytime now, cross the Rhein River and liberate us. We had no appreciation of the size or strength of the German drive, nor did we know at this point that it was an all-out life and death struggle offensive for them. They were determined to break the back of the Allied Offensive and turn the tide of the war in their favor.

In our limited space and understanding we had already begun to be more concerned with our own survival than the war. We were struggling with hunger, inadequate clothing, shock, cold, and inhuman treatment. The population was hostile toward us and we had no hope of help from them regarding food, shelter, or compassion. It was interesting to note that the Northern Germans were extremely hostile toward us, spitting on us as we would pass groups of them, shouting obscenities at us, and even throwing objects at us; while the Southern Germans, as we found later, were more compassionate and apt to help us whenever it was safe for them to do so. One has to consider, however, that we encountered the Southern Germans months later, and much nearer the end of the war when they had finally realized that defeat was imminent.

Early in the morning of the second or third day of walking, we heard the strange haunting sound of bagpipes floating over the column. We were puzzled as to the source of this music but soon learned that an Army Colonel who also had been captured had always carried bagpipes with him in battle as a hobby and had managed to salvage them even in the heat of battle. It seems that he was using them to lead us, and seemingly trying to unite us in our thinking and establish an *Esprit de Corps* which was badly needed. We later learned that he was the ranking officer and the one the Germans used in an attempt to maintain order and get their major points across to us. In general, we all felt strangely reassured by this and felt more of a unit than at any time previously. It seems always to take a disaster to unite opposing forces, overcome petty differences and stiffen the camaraderie necessary for survival. At this point we were still fairly well civilized and apt to share cigarettes, extra clothing and ideas, a situation which was to change drastically for the worse in the following weeks and months. This occurred in direct proportion to the increased cold, hunger, and fatigue. The basic survival drive was insidiously rearing its head. An example of this was when some of the men who knew a little German had learned that the German word for "hot" is "heiss" but did not share this knowledge with others who were not aware of it. This only becomes important when you realize that in extreme cold, anything hot, even water, can be vital. These men had been getting hot water from farmhouses as we progressed, with the rest of us thinking that " heiss " meant cold and avoiding any offer of this "cold water"; thinking how dumb the others were to introduce anything cold into their bodies - we were using snow for our fluid bulk. After we learned the truth, it got to be a dog-eat-dog effort to get to the " heiss " water first.

The relief of being away from the battlefront, and in less danger was counteracted by a growing awareness that we were beginning to wear down and getting on each other's nerves more and more. The distance we had traveled was pointed out to us when the German Guard Company accompanying us had to be relieved by another because the guards were unable to keep up the pace of 20 miles a day, even though they had been eating regularly, while we had not. Our guards were men who could not be in battle and as a result were not physically capable of maintaining any rigorous activity for a long time. At this point we were still in fairly good physical condition and seemed to be able to handle the situation adequately. The German Guard was utilizing contact with farms, along with their own daily rations to maintain their diet. They had none to share with us. In a way this made us feel superior to them, which in our own American way always had been true, but in another way it all seemed so very unfair. For a while our spirits were up but our stomachs were still empty and the morale boost was short lived.

Small towns came and went. There seemed to be no goal but always there was talk of a train ride which in itself began to have value as a goal and would help us get through the endless foot-in-front-of-a-foot miles we were covering.

Chapter 2

About 5 days after we had been captured and after we had already walked about 100 miles, two unexpected and frightening events occurred deepening our insecurity; making it quite clear that we had no control whatsoever about our treatment or destiny.

There had been talk of the possible use of poison gas in the German offensive action against the Allies. This had been discussed by the guards who had been responsible for us. The rumors went from one end of our long straggly line of men to the other end. The use of poison gas had of course been outlawed but then who makes and keeps the rules in a life and death struggle situation like a war? Using us as prisoners, and seemingly as hostages, in an attempt to prevent retaliation on the part of the Allies for their use of poison gas; the German guards ordered us to throw away our gas masks. Any refusal to do so was considered an act of rebellion and punishable by being shot. Now we were stripped of a vital protective piece of equipment and did not hesitate to let our feelings be known. We began swearing at the guards at the top of our lungs but to no avail. Our pleading and shouting fell on deaf ears. We continued to grumble in true American style. Our outburst was followed by another order to throw away all of our mess gear (eating equipment), knives, forks, spoons, cups and aluminum plates. Again we protested in the loudest possible manner but again there was no relenting. This time the guards showed irritation, began to threaten us and even struck some of the louder protestors. The unbelievable clatter of metal being thrown down expressed quite well our resentment and hostility toward the guards and the loss of our equipment. Except for the knives there seemed to be no justification for taking away our own means of obtaining or preparing food even if we should ever be able or lucky enough to locate any.

Shortly after stripping us of the equipment, we were led into what appeared to be an old abandoned makeshift prison camp. The buildings were falling down from lack of maintenance, the barbed wire enclosures were falling down and the buildings lacked paint. Even the stairs approaching the buildings were broken. Siding had been ripped off or blown away so that protection from the wind was minimal. By now the temperature had fallen well below the freezing mark and the winds were gusting up to 40 miles per hour, making the chill factor devastating.

We were lined up outside the buildings in long rows and allowed to enter only a few at a time. Once inside, the bleakness was even more overwhelming. There were a few tables scattered around and there were German officers or possibly administrative help seated at these tables. In an adjoining room there was a shower and what appeared to be a team of medical personnel.

We were told to empty our pockets of everything, and put the contents on the table while one soldier went through the items, taking each piece of paper out of our wallets, including our medical records, pictures of family, driver's licenses and so on. Another was asking questions such as "your name", "your rank", "your army unit", "where were you captured" and on and on. All that is required according to the Geneva Convention is that you gave your Name, Rank and Serial Number; which of course is what we did. It is one thing to learn this procedure in a training situation during basic training in the United States and quite another to be facing an enemy who does everything in his power to degrade and intimidate you. Some of us, Captains and above, were taken into another more comfortable office filled with filing cabinets, a makeshift desk and some chairs. The occupants of this room were a German Captain and a couple of armed guards. The Captain spoke perfect English and put on a show of being amiable in his communication with us. The amazing thing about this encounter was when he pulled a rather complete file on some of us, knowing where we had been born, our age, parents' names and even schools we had attended. He was quick and proud to announce that he had spent much time in the United States prior to the war, in such places as Buffalo, New York, Cleveland, Ohio and several other places. We were inclined to suspect that this was a set up to gain our confidence or give the impression that there was nothing we could tell him that he did not already know but we did not make a point of challenging him with this suspicion.

The Captain then chose to talk to each of us alone, going into great detail about our background and, in my case, telling me that my grandparents had left Germany in 1882, which was a fact; even knowing that they came from Dresden, Germany. He then proceeded to question me about my loyalty to the "Fatherland", asking how I could join the Americans against my "Homeland" and fight my own people. He said that this disloyalty was going to result in my being on the losing side. I stated that I did not feel that this was the case but he cut me short and offered a proposal which I'm sure he thought I could not refuse. He told me that if I joined the German Army my post would be in Berlin where I would enjoy "wine", "women" and "song" for the duration of the war and that I could then become a German citizen. He ranted and raved about my stupidity when I told him the whole idea was crazy. He said he would give me time to reconsider. I assured him that there would be no consideration at all. He then summoned another officer who apparently got the same treatment as I had gotten and with the same results.

I was taken back to the interrogation room, and told to remove all of my clothing. The room was full of naked men who were very cold, had been searched, and were waiting to be told what to do next. In an attempt to save their wrist watches, most of the men had hidden them in various places such as the lining of their coats, in their combat boots, and any other place they could think of. One after the other I watched the guards find the hidden watches and decided to try "The Purloined Letter" approach and leave mine on my wrist. Surprisingly this worked, and I walked out wearing my watch which I have with me to this very day.

After the search we were taken to the shower room and told to bathe, which was the least likely thing that we would want to do in this 15 degree temperature with the wind howling through the cracks, never seeming to let up. We did comply, as there was little else we could do. Half frozen but clean, we were permitted to dress, except for our undershirts, the reason for which we soon understood. We were ushered into a room with a medical team, where one after the other we watched them plunge a hypodermic needle into the breast of each soldier. We asked what the shot was for but they pretended not to understand the question or perhaps they really didn't. One subordinate officer mumbled in broken English that we would know in 20 years what the shot was for. He would not elaborate. Even though this seemed to be an unbelievable length of time to wait for the results of an experiment, we were also aware that he might be referring to a futuristic annihilation of Americans, through failure to be able to reproduce or even unthinkable setting up a physical deterioration in those of us who might survive. While rumors ran rampant through the group, a German doctor announced in broken English that the shot was to prevent Typhus, a much feared disease in Germany at this time. We were left to take our choice of believing him or giving way to rumor. Most of us chose to believe him, largely to allay our fear and anxiety about the whole situation. To this day, however, a thin line of doubt still persists.

A positive outcome of this experience at this abandoned camp was that we were permitted to stay indoors, sleeping on the wooden floor for the remainder of the night. This was our first time indoors to sleep and we thought of that as a luxury at this time; although would not have thought of it as a luxury a week ago.

The following morning we were "rousted" out before dawn to continue our march in the ever-increasing fall of snow, with temperatures dropping daily. The long, winding, snake-like column of soldiers had now raised the numbers to about 6,000. We had lost some men along the way when they were shot for falling too far behind in the line, had just given up hope or were suffering from unattended wounds which finally infected and killed them. We didn't always know what happened to others, nor did we know what their problems were, nor did the guards encourage any long range communication between us. Some men may have escaped, although we would not get word to this effect since it would create new alertness on the part of the German guards and possibly bring a reprisal on those of us who were still in captivity.

There was little to occupy the time as we moved; except to get better acquainted with the men nearest you in the line. Not all friends were together. It was a rare privilege when you saw someone you had known and were able to start the next day's march with him. While many of us were in the same unit of the Army prior to capture, we were separated during all of the confusion of battle and the subsequent escape from machine gun slaughter. It constantly ran through my mind that a childhood buddy I had admired had been shot down over Germany two years prior to this time and I wondered if it would ever be possible to run across him in a country as large as this, under these circumstances - the chances seemed very slim.

Although the weather had gotten very cold, and there was much snow from time to time, the visibility in the sky was such that the Allied planes, fighters and bombers were able once again to take to the air. While this was a comforting thought, because to our minds this brought us close to the end of the war and our liberation, we had not reckoned with the fact that while on the ground and seen from the air, our pilots did not know us from the German troops who might be moving to new positions. Our first taste of reality of our plight came suddenly at dawn of the 8th day. We were cheering loudly because we had spotted the plane as one of ours, but the pilot had no way of knowing we were prisoners of war, and as a result came in with guns blazing, strafing the entire length of the column. Instinctively we moved to the left and right out of the line of fire, but the slower and less lucky men were killed outright or wounded. As fate would have it we lost surprisingly few men on that pass but we quickly came to the conclusion that we had to do something before the plane returned or another one showed up. A command decision, by several of us, quickly rallied the men into a huge, human POW, the initials for Prisoners of War, which could be seen from the air. You have never seen men move so fast, nor obey orders so quickly. Everyone knew something had to be done fast. The success of that maneuver was apparent when the next plane coming in on us hesitated, banked to the right, waggled his wings, and best of all did not shoot at us. It became immediately apparent to us that he communicated this information to others because from that point on planes looked us over before shooting and, on seeing our POW made of soldiers, would waggle wings and move on. The German guards did not object to this maneuver because it offered them the same protection we were getting.

Not much later in the war, however, we were forbidden, by order of the German High Command to form our POW. Evidently they wanted to confuse our pilots who were shooting at everything on the ground that moved except POW groups. There was a rumor that German soldiers were using the same idea of POW with their foot soldiers in order to avoid being strafed by Allied planes. As a result of not being able to protect ourselves, the loss of men was tragically increased as we proceeded to what was now referred to as our entraining point; to be moved further into Germany and presumably to a Prisoner of War Camp.

The loss of our ability to form our POW was devastating to our morale. Any planes, now even at a distance, brought fear to our hearts. This carried on for months after the war was over and after I had returned to Akron, Ohio, my hometown. I was dressed up in a suit and walking in a downtown area in Akron, when an unthinking, stupid pilot, buzzed the main street. Still reacting as I had in Germany months before, I moved to my right which put me in the middle of the street and fell flat on my face, covering my head. I was embarrassed as I saw the reaction of dozens of people who were looking on.

Stalag IXB near Bremen. This camp was liberated in April 1945.

German Soldier in winter gear, c.1942
Image courtesy Keith Ward

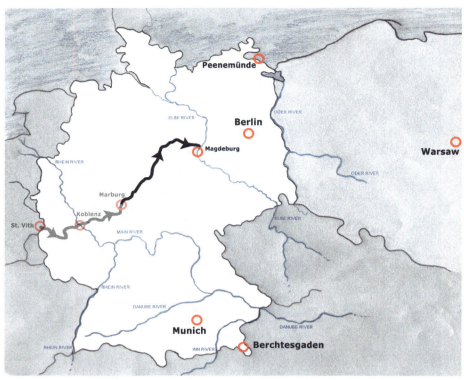

German soldiers on a train, c.1940
The writing is from the marching song "Das Engellandlied" by Hermann Löns.
The chalked lyrics reference leaving a sweetheart to fight England.
Image courtesy Keith Ward

Chapter 3
CRISIS OVER TRAIN TRAVEL

On the days following our interrogation, bathing and being stripped of our last possessions; we were marching along in an uneventful, boring manner. The countryside was bleak because it was winter but the knowledge that we were in a foreign country brought with it a kind of excitement that we might see something new and different, instead of just the back of the soldier in front of us. The feeling which kept us going was that just over the next hill a town might appear or there might be a farmhouse offering food to our hungry mob or we might even see the train which we were now anticipating seeing at any time. It was going to be a relief to ride for a while and have food brought to us, hopefully hot food to remove some of the chill from our bones. Our hope of getting on a train and riding was a very real vitalizing goal which seemed to make the walking easier and the cold and hunger easier to bear.

About noon we were treated to the long awaited sight. The train really was there just ahead; just standing and waiting for the approximately 6,000 foot-weary, hungry soldiers to get aboard and be taken to civilization, where they didn't forget to feed you and provide a bunk for our weary bones. Perhaps I am being a little hard on the German guard contingency. They didn't really have any way to get food for this many men and no one in the high command of the German Army seemed to care one way or the other. In Spartan fashion, we accepted the resulting pain of it all. It was easy to forgive all of the misery we had endured when the train was in sight. We began to joke and our spirits being much lighter. Even the cold didn't seem so bad and we were certain that in a small country like Germany we would rather quickly be at an Army Post, a Prison Camp or some facility where they could take care of us properly. The thrill of anticipation produced more out and out adrenalin and we were literally running toward the train. The engine of the train was rather small by American standards but we were more concerned when we noted that there were not many cars attached to it. From what we could count of the cars and knowing that there were about 6,000 of us, we soon realized that we were not going to be riding in great comfort. Still a little discomfort was better than walking and definitely faster. We were lined up and herded into the cars which had only the usual sliding doors of a cattle car for an opening. Those of us who went in first soon found ourselves literally crushed against the back wall of the car and having to stand up. There were so many men in each car there was no way you could either sit or fall down. After what seemed to be an endless period of time and with our tendency to claustrophobia mounting, we heard a shout, evidently that all was clear, because we began to move. What a glorious sensation, moving without trying. I have to say one good thing about being packed in the cars as tight as we were, we were really warm for the first time in many days and had hope. If you could just remember that the ultimate goal, not the present discomfort, was all that mattered, it was possible to endure this whole miserable situation. Thoughts of food and warmth and rest dominated our minds, little else mattered.

As the clatter of the wheels on the tracks rhythmically passed the time and a kind of hypnotic trance came over the men, we were suddenly alerted to the roar of an engine, louder than the train engine, seeming to come from ahead of us. This shook us from our trance and we realized with renewed fear, one thing we had never considered in our joy of traveling. The one thing we had never been exposed to before, the reality of an air attack while being imprisoned in a boxcar We were like rats in a trap and at the mercy of whatever would transpire. The groans of disbelief and fear were loud, our claustrophobia became unbearable but was short lived because almost as soon as we had heard the first plane, a second one came at us in a steep dive with all machine guns spitting fire and bullets everywhere. Men screamed in agony and pain, some just stood in abject fear and others began to pray aloud. I felt a dull thud on my shoulder, but in the confusion, and fear of another strafing, I paid no attention to it. Suddenly the train stopped, throwing us forward, nearly crushing the men in the front of the car, the doors were thrown open. Men started to detrain, falling out of the door, pushed by those behind them, everyone scrambling out any way they could, trying not to fall on or walk on others but getting as far away from the train as they could. It was only after we were out of the cars and feeling safe that we were aware of how devastating just one pass of an airplane strafing had been. Some men just fell forward and did not move. Others were holding their heads, their sides, their legs and their arms, trying to stem the flow of the blood spurting out or flowing everywhere. Men appeared to be in shock or pain, it was difficult to tell which. I was suddenly aware that I wasn't feeling anything in my left arm, nor was I able to lift it. I was sure it had been shot off or that there would be a hole in it - but surprisingly it was there, and there was no blood. All of this passed through my mind in less time than it took to tell it. What had really happened was a bullet had come through the panel of the wooden boxcar just above my shoulder height where I had been pressed against the wall, then it deflected upward and hit my shoulder like a sledgehammer, not breaking the skin or even causing it to bleed. Later I realized my shoulder was black and blue and it was a week before I could use it again. Others were not so lucky and a total of 800 men were killed or wounded in that one pass of a plane which turned out to be British, not American as we had first thought.

As quickly as we were out of the train we formed our trusty POW made up of men who could still walk or run into position. The planes must have seen us then and realized what happened. They made a couple of low flying passes without shooting, waggled their wings and moved on, following the train tracks to the southwest.

To add to the tragedy of our situation, the train commander would not allow the train to move, kept us well away from it and could do nothing for the dead or wounded. After keeping us out in the field for an hour he announced that he would again entrain us. To his dismay and I am sure disbelief, not one soldier in our group would even get on the train. He threatened to have us shot but at this time everyone was in such shock, so hungry, tired, and cold, that nobody really gave a damn what he did and we told him so. The German guards, some of whom had been wounded, had a conference with the train commander and it was decided to put the dead and wounded on the train and let it continue without the rest of us. While this confab and decision making was going on, we heard heavy bombers overhead flying to the northeast. We identified them as American B-25's and were jubilant feeling that the war was again continuing in the air and hopefully shortening our captivity time. The planes were at about 30,000 feet altitude and we were not in fear of them as we had been of the fighter planes. At such heights bombers do not have visual contact with targets and we knew we were not significant enough targets for them anyway.

Immediately upon hearing the bombers, we were made aware that we were indeed back in a war zone. German anti-aircraft guns began firing on the bombers. The sky was full of black smoke, exploding shells, surrounding the bombers with deadly accuracy. It was like a bad dream or should I say a nightmare. Here we were standing by a railroad track, still in the shock over our own devastation and there were our planes being blasted literally out of the sky by anti-aircraft guns. We were watching them in the sky in awe, barely able to comprehend the significance of it all until we saw one of the bombers explode in mid-air, thousands of feet above us. Parts of the plane were scattered all over the sky, amidst thousands of bundles of aluminum foil they had dropped to thwart radar detection. We watched one entire wing of an airplane descend to earth. It seemed to be in slow motion as it spun like a propeller. The largest portion of the fuselage of the plane ejected several tiny dots which turned out to be those of the crew who managed to free themselves. As they drifted down they were targets for ground snipers and some were unlucky enough to be caught in the ack-ack fire of the anti-aircraft guns. A couple of men made it down and were immediately taken into custody and added to our group of prisoners. They were probably lucky because many airmen in similar distress had been taken by a hostile civilian population who had just undergone a bombing and were very angry and would beat or kill the airmen without compassion.

While all of this was happening I couldn't help but wonder if my brother Bob, who was in the Air Corps flying missions in this area, might have been up there. I learned later that the chances were good that he had been and that while flying missions and knowing I had been captured, would often drop a package of clothing, socks, gloves and canned foods, in a futile hope that I might somehow get it. Amidst all of this I was feeling sorrier for the poor men in the planes who were sitting ducks for anti-aircraft fire, than I was for those of us relatively safer on the ground.

The din of explosions northeast of us indicated that we were probably not too far from an important town or possibly a large city and we had hoped that perhaps we could still get to some kind of civilization soon. By this time we didn't know where we were or how far we had come from the entraining point. We did know that we were heading generally east and the town of Magdeburg was mentioned by the guards.

We walked for a few miles following all of the events of the day and were bedded down as usual, on the ground, with nothing to keep us warm but the proximity of another soldier. We were near a farmhouse and the guards who were not actually on duty were bedded down in a nearby barn, having eaten a fairly good meal prepared by an unwilling farm woman. I say unwilling, because at this point in the war, rations of food were getting very short in Germany and the appearance of a couple hundred guards and prisoners was not really a welcome sight to the farmers. After finishing their meals, some of the more compassionate guards would offer any nearby prisoner the scraps of food from his plate. Not many prisoners were lucky enough to be that nearby, and I for one always seemed to be in the wrong place or too late in the right place.

Arising at dawn and continuing our march, it wasn't long until Magdeburg loomed into view. It was a fair sized town and showed the scars of having been bombed, with some whole blocks of rubble still in evidence where old style buildings once had stood. The streets of the town were fairly wide and people were walking, probably to work; occasionally shouting an obscenity at us or using what was to be often heard by us, the phrase, "American gangsters from Chicago."

The most memorable sight and also the most heartbreaking was seeing a large plate glass window in a butcher shop with frankfurters piled up in it and we were just marched by it. The unfairness of it all. It was like rubbing our noses in our plight and yet I can't believe that this was done on purpose or with malice or forethought. Magdeburg came and went and we saw the city fade behind us as we now headed east, south of Berlin, toward Warsaw, Poland. We were told that there was an Oflag (a camp for officers) there and that we were to be kept there for the duration of the war.

City square of Hildesheim, Germany, April 7, 1945
The city fell to the 2nd Armored Division of the 9th US Army in April 1945.
Photographed by Pfc. D. C. Rekoske, U.S. National Archives SC 335309

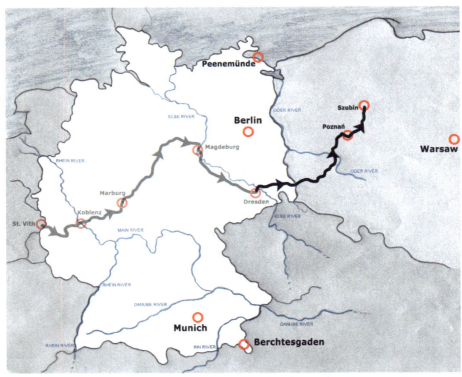

A Nazi officer eating a can of C-rations in the ruins of Saarbrucken, Germany west of Kaiserslautern, 1945.
Image courtesy National Archives (535981, 208-YE-145)

Chapter 4
WARSAW AND END OF TRIP - NO WAY

Being happy go lucky Americans and very optimistic, we figured that the worst had happened to us and now the march to the east and Warsaw would be just something to get out of the way - how wrong we were. We were not really sophisticated enough in the ways of war and fortune to realize that we were in a unique position, being able to see a country go down in defeat, getting a first-hand view of what the Germans went through as they saw their towns destroyed, their homes threatened and often bombed out from under them and feeling the wrath they had toward us when they saw or learned that a loved one was hurt or killed. I remembered the reactions of my own men before we were captured when they learned that a brother of one of our men was killed the day before. They were ready to maim and kill the next German soldier captured and it took a direct command order to stop this kind of senseless killing.

We would be passing through areas from which the Germans were firing their infamous V-1 and V-2 rockets aimed at the Allies and Britain killing soldiers and civilians indiscriminately. We would see the change in attitude of the German people toward their leaders and their lack of response to Hitler's impassioned speeches on the radio after it was evident that defeat was imminent. As these events unfolded I never ceased to be aware of the unique opportunity afforded by all of the rare insights to be gained in being behind enemy lines and fluid in the situation. We could hear radios blasting out Hitler's voice imploring his people to fight to the end, demanding loyalty from them, promising success of the war effort but saying it was only with the full cooperation of all German people working in concerted efforts that they were to thwart the enemy. He assured them that he would be in Berlin, directing all war efforts. There was mixed reaction on the part of the people hearing these broadcasts and some even made fun of his hysterical voice and the tone of his speeches.

We would be seeing people going through their own lives in small towns, as though nothing else was happening, seeming to be unaware of the war. We would see frightened people, crippled soldiers, children's camps, long columns of men. We would be seeing artillery firing literally over our heads, in both directions, sometimes simultaneously, going toward both the Allied and German troops.

At times I felt that I was totally crazy. I'm sure my buddies thought so; because I was seeing our whole situation as an adventure, albeit not voluntarily entered into. It was an unequalled, once-in-a-lifetime opportunity to see new countries, war at intermittent intervals, destruction and beauty blended in a confusion of emotions, on the part of all concerned.

Chapter 4

The weather was getting worse, the temperature continued to drop, and the snow was piling up, at times as much as 3 or 4 feet. We had adjusted to the foot-in-front-of-a-foot routine, and learned a kind of self-hypnosis to block out much of the reality of the bitter cold and the excessive hunger but the full force of reality often came breaking through our best defenses. Many of us developed a higher pain tolerance and seemed able to handle an excess of extremes; while others seemed to be more sensitive to the cold and literally gave up, just sitting down, refusing to move any further and some dying this way. There was one such incident in which one of my best friends Bill and I decided that there was no point in going on. We discussed our total dismal situation in what we considered was a realistic manner, weighing the pros and cons of dying. After due consideration, we tabled a decision at this point.

After endless days of walking in a vast wasteland of snow, flat windswept country, freezing snow, with nothing to break the monotony of seeming to go nowhere, we reconsidered quitting. At night after a 10 to 20 mile walk, we would huddle close to each other on the ground, burrow into a snow bank to break the ever blowing, howling wind, with a chill factor of 10 to 30 degrees below zero. After going through such a night, we would again be rousted out to continue on the next day. The only change in our routine was that one night our feet had finally frozen, turned black up to the knee, and lacked any feeling. We agreed with each other that if we were not to be left behind or, even worse, be taken somewhere to have our legs amputated by hostile German doctors, we had better thaw out our feet and legs ourselves. We knew that circulation was the key and so all that night long we reinforced each other in the ritual of stomping and rubbing our feet, thus restoring circulation. It worked, because we did not lose one man because of frozen feet, although I am sure that night there were many circulation problems set up for future toes, feet and legs.

Not long after this episode, my friend Bill and I again compared our view points on whether or not we were going to be able to survive the lack of food, the bitter cold and the constant energy drain the long march was creating. We calmly came to the conclusion that we could not. We had heard how easy it is to freeze to death, how you really feel very warm just before dying and decided the alternative was attractive. During one break we sat by the side of the road, closed our eyes to die. The howling wind was whipping around my legs and I kept feeling a hard object persistently bumping against the calf of my leg. Reaching down idly I felt a rectangular shaped object inside the lining of my trench coat. Without any particular emotion I tore the coat open and to my amazement out dropped an Army D bar. An Army D bar is a highly concentrated, nutritional kind of candy bar with chocolate. It was like a sign from a Supreme Energy, saying, "Don't give up" or "Even when things are the worst, I am still with you." "Eat, and get up and get going." I broke the bar in half, gave half to Bill and ate the other half. Never before had anything tasted as good as that dry, cold and old candy bar. When the march resumed, we got up and went along, never again to feel desperate enough to even consider quitting or dying. We were now determined that we would live unless the Germans made pointed efforts aimed at killing us. Survival had triumphed again but the near brush with dying gave much cause for soul searching about the meaning of life and a reassessment of values.

We had already walked through Christmas Eve and Christmas Day. Our only contact with the reality of Christmas was when we were walking along the ridge of a very high hill looking down into a valley very late Christmas Eve. We could see a small church lit only by candles. The faint sound of a German choir singing Silent Night, seemed to reach out to us. The sound of the church bells could be heard long after we had passed this scene and the nostalgia rose in us to an almost unbearable level. We were feeling sorry for ourselves and worrying about those back home who did not even know what had happened to us. Our spirits were lower than the floor of the valley.

Continuing our course for Warsaw we saw, coming in the opposite direction, another column of men. They even looked more pitiful than we did which was bad enough. Their feet were bound up in rags, their clothing was in tatter, their faces were gaunt, and they were filthy and dirty; looking for the most part like a column of hollow eyed zombies. We passed close to them and could tell they were Russians from hearing them talk. One man held out his hand and called out in a weak voice begging, "cigarettes." I could not stand to deny him this request, even though my own supply of cigarettes, used for trading was nearly exhausted. I soon realized that the Germans did not take kindly to such a compassionate gesture and as soon as I had thrown the cigarette to the man, I was knocked to the ground by the German colonel in charge of the Russian column. He began to curse me and his tirade seemed to feed itself. He took out his pistol, a very mean looking German Luger, shoved the end of the barrel into my mouth and said he was going to kill me. I began to sweat and shake in panic and decided there was nothing I could do but die at that point when suddenly a shout from his own marching group caused him to turn and run rapidly to the head of his column thereby saving my life. As he withdrew the pistol he gave me a final vicious shove, leaving me completely drained of all energy and badly shaken up.

We later learned that these Russians had been captured early in the German-Russian conflict and were being returned from the Russian front near Warsaw where they had served as work crews in preparing defenses in and around Warsaw. They were being shifted to the western front for similar purposes, but from the looks of them few of them would ever make the move successfully.

One of the methods that we ingenious Americans utilized to survive was through fantasy. It was quite obvious we had no food, but we had good memories and so one day we decided that each man would spend as much time as he could possibly take to give his favorite recipe for his favorite food. This was later expanded to each man who was participating, to have him describe his favorite place to eat or the most fantastic restaurant he had ever visited. Smorgasbord restaurants had just been introduced in America and provided the basis for some of the most outlandish descriptions of varieties and selection of foods that it is possible to imagine. Jim, a tall gaunt looking man with a slight southern accent was the first to start. He described a place called Fettrow's, which was located somewhere near Columbus, Ohio, where the Prime Rib of Beef was so tender that it would melt in your mouth. The selections from the Smorgasbord table were unlimited and the quantities were voluminous. Jim's description of "fresh fish," "succulent pork," and "rare beef" stimulated visual and olfactory images. There were many vegetables to choose from and each was described in detail. He sometimes took an hour to just describe the making of a cheese sauce or a gravy. You must understand that no one was ever in a hurry to end their recipe; because we were all savoring every last morsel of this imaginary food and participating in its preparation. At times the fantasy was so real, the description so vivid and detailed, that we could taste the food - the contented smiles on our face must have confused our guards at times.

We then were taken by another soldier to a place in St. Louis where there were rare foods, exotic dishes prepared on our order as you sat there. Of course, everyone wanted to be sure to remember this one but unfortunately the soldier telling the story could not remember the name of the place. Naturally, everyone was disappointed and downcast but at least knew that it was in St. Louis and promised to look it up "when we get home." Then there was the Stockyard Restaurant in Chicago, Illinois, where you picked your choice steak from a mound of ice piled high with all of the different cuts of steak and then you branded your steak with your initials just like in the old west. The thought of the branding iron, glowing red hot had the effect of warming us. We must not forget the place in Skeiniatlas, New York, (Skaneateles) at least that's how Ed thought it was spelled, where they had a choice of 7 different kinds of meats and fish, every known vegetable and desserts of every possible description. Chocolate Mousse, Jello, Butterscotch pudding, cakes, pies of all kinds, hot rum sauces and your choice of any kind of hot beverage known to man. Perhaps a slight exaggeration but then who cared at this point. When it came my turn, I felt very plain; because during all of my experience as a Prisoner of War, my only fantasy was of hamburger sandwiches with pickle, mustard and onion with a hot cup of coffee with thick cream in it. I was haunted by this thought night and day, to the point that when I returned to the United States, my first act was to eat 6 hamburgers and drink 5 cups of coffee. The restaurant owner finally refused to serve me anymore, possibly thinking I might die from overeating.

So that I would not let my friends down, I decided to describe one of my favorite meals in detail - cornbread and beans with a tossed salad. The beans must be of the Great Northern variety, must be cooked very slowly on low heat for hours, and must, of course, be cooked with just the right amount of onion and a ham butt or ham hock according to your own taste. The cornbread has to be light with just enough sugar to keep any trace of bitterness from appearing. The dressing for the salad has to be a delicate blend of vinegar, sugar, cream, and Miracle Whip salad dressing. The salad is tomato, lettuce, onion and cucumber, coated with the special dressing. All of this is topped off with a fresh cup of coffee with heavy cream.

Surprisingly these fantasy trips of cooking, visiting restaurants and making up recipes or using actual useable recipes, kept us so enthralled that we were able to forget our plight, forget the cold for hours on end and I feel that this was the greatest contributor to our survival during this period of the bleak march to Warsaw.

As we approached Warsaw, we were again reminded of the war and the screams of the shells as they passed overhead on their way to deliver death and destruction to the Russians to the east. Planes were overhead and we continued our struggle to get out of the way of strafing. The planes grew fewer as we approached Poland and the Russian front.

At one point we passed what looked like a launching pad for the V-1 or the V-2 rockets, which the Germans had been able to develop and get into the air. They were significantly ahead of the Allies in rocketry. Suddenly there was a roar, a flash of fire and the huge casing started to rise into the air, slowly at first but then with increasing velocity. We were in awe and we had never experienced anything like this noise, nor this view and it was extremely frightening. Here we were amidst the source of the deadly missiles, unable to do anything to stop the launching of these giants of destruction being used against our friends and allies. We ourselves had not long ago been on the receiving end of these monsters while in England. We had seen the huge craters when a whole building disappeared on impact. The disruption of communications and the frequent fires were etched in our memories. The frustration here was that there was absolutely nothing we could do to stop the missiles nor let anybody know that we knew where the launching pad was. The city of Peenemunde had been mentioned but held little meaning for us.

The German guard company had again changed. We had outlasted our third guard company by this time. Sometime around the 12th of January we finally saw the city of Warsaw and thought that our ordeal was finished. We were the first of Allied troops to see this magnificent city, albeit the worse for having been ravaged by bombs and battles. The Polish people were compassionate and as much as they dared to, would stand along our route of march trying to give us items of food, bread, onion, eggs or anything else they could hand us but in doing so they literally risked their lives. The guards would actually knock them away with rifle butts or threaten to shoot them for trying to help us. It was wonderful to feel compassion and love here in Poland contrasted with the hate and anger we had directed at us in Germany. We were quickly marched to the northeast to an Oflag; this for officers, as contrasted to Stalag for enlisted men.

The scene was bleak and barren. Rows of wooden building enclosed in barbed wire, with disheveled looking men milling about the yard, aimlessly looking us over as we approached. The feeling as we entered the camp was one of mixed emotion - it marked the end of a march which had been total hell, yet we were now for the first time to realize that we would be surrounded by barbed wire fence and truly locked up for the first time. This goes against the American grain and we were very depressed. On the other hand, we knew that at least they have food here, that we would be fed and have a place to sleep. There was also the plus factor that the Red Cross would know where we were and could supplement our food with Red Cross packages. This turned out to be much less than expected. The Germans in charge of distribution of the packages seemed to "lose" some of the packages along the route to us and, as a result, a box of food meant for one soldier often had to be divided 16 ways. This meant that it did not do any one person a great deal of good but did provide us with some trading material in the form of cigarettes for which we were mighty grateful. This was the only time I can think of where anyone thought of cigarettes as good for your health.

A Prisoner of War Camp leaves much to be desired in every sense. It is bleak, dirty, confining, cold, damp, unpainted and placed row on row with isles or streets in between. The towers for the guards are placed in strategic locations giving full coverage to the compound below. Inside each building there was a potbellied stove with a pipe extended into the ceiling for a chimney, bunk-type crudely built wooden beds and straw filled burlap for mattresses. At least we finally had a blanket, although it proved inadequate for the cold of the building. Although there was a potbellied stove, there was not ample fuel for heating a building the size of the barracks, especially since the buildings were not insulated. Chilblains was a common problem. This is a condition where your feet feel frozen, get numb and ache like a toothache most of the time.

One of the first things the German soldiers did to us on arrival at the camp was to delouse us. The delousing process is one in which you are to remove all of your clothing, walk through a tunnel-like room where you are sprayed with water in a shower like apparatus and then a powder is sprayed on you coming from an apparatus much like a fire extinguisher. Body lice was a serious and common problem wherever larger groups of people, soldiers, or civilians were gathered. You have no idea what it is like to have lice until you have felt a louse or lice running from the back of your head down your stomach or back, under your belt, then on down your leg and then return. We were grateful for this treatment.

Following the "medical treatment" we were assigned to a barracks and finally given our first official meal, this being the first week in January. The meal consisted of a slice of bread, which had literally a sawdust base and was very grainy. We also had one spoonful of cottage cheese, one spoonful of some unfamiliar tasting jelly, one potato and a small cup of beef barley soup. The Ersatz coffee, which is powdered burnt barley grain dissolved in hot water, was given to us and except for its heat value, we would not have even drunk it.

To show how quickly soldiers can adjust and relax, even under adverse conditions, consider the following. We were sitting around toasting our bread on the stove pipes (which I will describe later), when we noticed that one man was cutting his slices paper thin. When we asked how he did this, he confided to us that he had secretly kept a scalpel he had been using when he was captured and had successfully kept it hidden all of this time. It turned out that he was a doctor in a field hospital which had been overrun, even though they are usually a safe distance from the front lines - this further demonstrating the depth of the German penetration during the Battle of the Bulge. As we discussed his profession with him it seems he had been a plastic surgeon before coming into the army. While we talked to him he had been looking at me curiously, then stated, "I could do something about that big nose of yours after the war is over, just a snip here and a snip there, and it would look great." All of this, under our present circumstance was bizarre, and I told him I would have to give such a project much consideration since I was not unhappy with my nose the way it was. I took a good deal of good natured ribbing after this episode with friends saying "John you'd better be careful what the doctor snips off," etc.

Chapter 4

As we soon got into the spirit of limited rations, we learned that it was possible to make the bread more palatable by placing it on the stove pipe leading through the roof and burning out some of the sawdust. This was not entirely sanitary but neither was most of the things we had done in the past weeks anyway. It did help the taste of the bread. In all honesty I have to admit that what they had given us to eat that day was to us akin to nectar for the Gods after what we had been through.

The organization in a prison camp is definite, though far from luxurious. There are days for showers, although the water is generally cold, there are no facilities nor equipment for shaving, unless you had had the foresight to bring a razor which of course none of us had had the opportunity to do. We now had our first chance to see ourselves in a mirror, and I must admit it was somewhat of a shock. The extreme loss of weight had left us looking sallow and hollow cheeked but because of the fact we had grown beards and moustaches our weight loss was not as noticeable as it would be later. We had a chance to see our feet for the first time, and it was a shock when I saw the bunions on the sides of my little and big toes, extending out as much as a half an inch. The reason for this is that when you are issued combat boots in the Army you get a wider width than you normally wear so that when you have a full field pack on your back the weight will cause your feet to fill out the boots just right. In our case we did not have full packs and we had lost so much weight, we were literally swimming in our boots, rubbing callouses near our little and big toes. Even to this day it is difficult to get a proper fitting shoe.

Finally after settling in which only took the better part of a day, we learned that you are told when you can leave the barracks buildings, where you can go and that there is a definite curfew in the evening, by which time you must be back in your assigned building. In my usual question to everyone as we had progressed around our route I asked if anyone knew Bob, my friend from the Air Corps who had been captured 2 years earlier. To my utter amazement and disbelief, one man said, "Oh you mean Bob Scheible, yeah, he's in the next barracks." I ran over to the next building, shouting, "Is Bob Scheible here?" I heard my buddy call out, "John, thank God you've come to liberate us." What a blow to all and a miserable feeling inside of me when I had to tell him that I was just another one of the prisoners and not a liberator. Nevertheless, after all of that emotion, our reunion was one of the warmest experiences I have ever known. We spent so much time talking, comparing experiences and answering other prisoners questions that the time got away from me and the curfew was in force. Here I was, a new prisoner in a camp, in the wrong barracks with a curfew declared and with no way to get safely back to my own barracks - the German guard would shoot anyone caught in the yard after curfew on sight. I was petrified with fear, trying desperately to figure out what to do. One of the older, long term prisoners said that they could hide me until morning and then I could return to my own barracks. The reason for hiding me was that there is a head count every night at around 10 o'clock. While the guards would not miss me in my barracks because they did not have an accurate count on new prisoners yet, they would find an extra man in this barracks and this would create a chaotic condition for all the prisoners in this compound.

At 10 o'clock the guard appeared and started the count. I was hidden under a mattress on one of the top bunk beds, praying that they would not look there, scarcely daring to breathe or move and sweating profusely. The count went okay because when they got the correct number, they left. Besides fearing for my own safety, I was concerned that I might have created a very serious problem for those who had befriended me. The night passed however with no further incident and when we were rousted out the next morning I slipped back to the barracks to which I had been assigned, never having been missed. The next night, however, the story would have had an entirely different ending, for that morning we were accounted and assigned definite bunks, after which anyone missing would be searched for until found. The result possibly being shot or at least punished in some manner. The guards would assume any irregularity an attempt to escape and would act accordingly.

We were given a rare opportunity later in the day because we were permitted to write a letter home. To this point we had no way of knowing what our families back home knew and what they did not know and we virtually felt like nonentities. The rules, there were always rules with the Germans, were strict about what we could and could not say. We were to let the people at home know that we were alive "and being well cared for" and that was about all, except maybe to express how we missed them, loved them and to wish that we were home. The monitors of the letter writing left no doubt in our minds that the letters would be heavily edited and censored, even with all the rules and near threats, it was wonderful to know and feel that some connection with the outside world would be made through this letter writing. Somehow it took away the loneliness and the futility of the whole experience of being captured, hungry and in the hands of an enemy who had little or no love for us.

The feeling of finally settling into a routine situation generated by the events of the past two days was to be disrupted by a situation which, up to now, had only been a rumor. We had been aware of the rumbling of heavy guns in the east, a good distance from us, but since we were not immediately threatened shrugged off the implications. We did not know how quickly our total situation was going to change, nor did we know how it would change, not only for us but the entire Oflag and German contingency.

RAF Officers dormitory, Schubin Oflag XXI B (later Oflag 64) POW Camp
September 25, 1942
Courtesy International Committee of the Red Cross (ICRC) archives (V-P-HIST-0158906)

Entrance to Stalag II B, Hammerstein, Germany
November 24, 1942
Courtesy International Committee of the Red Cross (ICRC) archives (V-P-HIST-03520-16)

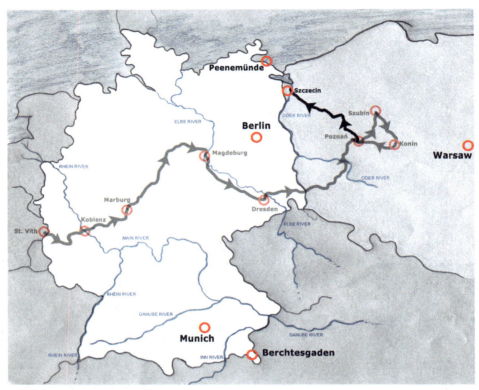

Oflag 64 prisoner certificate, 1945 (RG 242)
Image courtesy National Archives Collection of Foreign Records Seized

RETURN TO GERMANY VIA AN OCEAN VOYAGE - ON FOOT

In any large gathering of people, especially when denied access to the outside world, there are always rumors of a variety of topics. We had heard that the Allies had broken through on the Western front and that liberation was only a matter of a few days, which we found out later was only a wishful thinking story of a soldier who always professed to be "in the know." Contrary to this we had heard that the Allies had been pushed back to the English Channel as had happened at Dunkirk and was therefore at least believable. This turned out to be pure fiction invented by an over-zealous German patriot. The story that the Russians were on their way to Warsaw and consequently to our prison camp, circulated cautiously but with a more ominous overtone. When this was mentioned, the German guards looked genuinely worried and at times very frightened. There were stories of how brutally the Germans had treated the Russians in the assault on Russia and in the near victory short of Moscow.

We had our first-hand view of the brutality of the German guard, during our own march to Warsaw. The guards were terrified of the possibility of retaliation in the event that the Russians were successful in their drive toward Warsaw. Stories of a break through and repulsion of the threat persisted, when in fact no one really knew what was happening. The constant rumbling of the guns being fired by both the German Army and the Russians within our hearing, left little doubt that there would be no settling down to any routine activities in this camp.

Early on the third day since we had arrived at the Oflag, we were rousted by very nervous and frightened German guards, who were telling us we were to grab whatever we could to keep warm and to get ready to move out as quickly as possible shouting at us "schnell, schnell." There was confusion and near hysteria among the German soldiers, many seemingly conflicting orders were being shouted and the abject fear on the faces of the guards was apparent. We gathered that word had come down that the Russians had broken through the eastern front and were descending on Warsaw, which turned out to be true. It seemed that the only concern of the camp commander was to get us out of the area to prevent the Russians from liberating us and to save their own necks at the same time. Even now they persisted in wanting to keep us as hostages.

Loosely organized, but very carefully guarded we were herded out of the camp and headed in a westerly direction. It was extremely cold, the wind was howling, and in the half light of dawn the soldiers scampering everywhere, there was an unreal aspect to our very existence. The thought of going back out into that Polish flat country and resuming our previous hellish conditions was almost overwhelmingly depressing. The only hope that any of us had that made the situation bearable was that the Russian Army might succeed in overrunning the Germans and actually liberate us. We had no thought of the mechanics of how this would happen or how we might be killed along with German soldiers when they were overrun. After all, the Russian artillery had no way of sorting out the good guys from the bad guys, nor did we even know if they were aware that we were there. This set off a whole new set of fears for us. We too had heard how the Russians moved quickly, decisively and murderously on an enemy and wondered whether or not we would have time to tell them "hey we're on your side." With this thought we were almost willing to run with the Germans to anywhere where our position would be generally safer. Running, tripping, slipping and sliding and falling we were moved to the west toward an unknown destination. We could hear the roar of the artillery and the general battle getting closer and closer. We later learned that the Russians had indeed gotten to Warsaw and in holding up there had unwittingly allowed our group of guards and prisoners to get away from them. The battle was so close that at times we were walking through a corridor with German artillery going over our heads toward the Russians, and the Russian artillery going over our heads toward the Germans. Fortunately, neither of them were aiming at us but the scream of the shells was just as unnerving, we didn't know what anyone was shooting at.

It didn't take us long to realize that we were once again in the rut of a foot-in-front-of-a-foot routine, out in the open and blinded by the awful whiteness of the snow and the nothingness ahead of us. I don't believe that there is anything worse than not having any idea of a destination or feeling that your captors are in little better position. What made it worse was that we knew the effect of the cold and the hunger potentials which lay ahead. We had learned this from our not too remote previous experience of the weeks prior to this.

One of the things which struck us was the benefit we had derived from just those couple of days in the Oflag. This was really instrumental in helping us to make a better adjustment to our total situation. At least we had learned to cope with cold and hunger within reason and, what is more, we each now had a blanket, a luxury not true in our previous exposure and the lice were temporarily under control.

In typical American style we were perpetually optimistic that it was only a matter of a short time until the Russian Army would overtake us and our ordeal would be over. As we passed through small Polish villages we were aware that the attitude of the Polish people matched our optimism, and they were more open in their hostile attitude toward the German soldiers, often shouting obscenities at them and gleefully asking them how it felt to be on the run for a change. It was obvious that they knew much more of the total situation than we could surmise and were feeling confident that it was only a matter of time until they would be liberated from the long torturous German occupation and oppression.

Our guards were literally rushing us through town after town often going from before dawn to well after dark. We could still hear the sounds of battle behind us. The German Luftwaffe was active in desperate attempts to assist the ground troops. We could see them going to our north and also to the south indicating to us that the Russian advance was on a broad front and closing fast.

After 5 days at a point midway between Warsaw and Poznan we entered a small town which had been evacuated. Some said it was Koto, and others thought it was Konin, but in any event the German guards suddenly disappeared without any warning, leaving us to just mill about. Their departure was rapid and unexpected and our being left in this manner we were understandably confused as to where we were and what had happened. It suddenly dawned on us that we were free and just as suddenly we knew why. The Russians were attacking from the east and went right on past us.

What we saw was unbelievable. There were Russian soldiers on horseback, riding hard and in every way, except the uniforms, reminding us of our own Cowboys chasing Indians. They paid little attention to us, although they did seem to know that we were not Germans. They seemed intent on pushing their advantage at such a speed as to nearly trample us at times.

After we recovered from the shock of what had happened we began to cheer and hug each other scarcely believing that it was all real, we experienced feelings of euphoria that you feel after a victorious home ball game.

We began to search the town for food and any sign of anyone who might be able to tell us where we were and what had really happened, but we found no one. When we reached the center of town which was a kind of square we were amazed and delighted to see a huge hog hanging from a rack, head down, split wide open, and thoroughly cleaned as though ready for roasting or cutting up, either of which we would be happy to undertake as soon as possible. We wondered why the people who left the hog there had left in such a hurry, not taking such a valuable food with them. We would never learn this. We busied ourselves with planning what to do with the hog. We had two major things to consider, one to build a fire, and two to start cutting up the meat, meaning we had to find a knife. We had little idea about cooking, but knew enough to build a kind of rack to lay the pork on and to do the cooking slowly. We scrounged around for wood using anything we thought would burn without adverse flavor. One soldier found some matches in a house nearby, and soon we had a beautiful warming fire going. We had intended to let it burn down making a charcoal bed suitable for roasting the meat but this was not to happen. Some prisoners on the west edge of town screamed that the Russians were returning in full retreat with Germans close on their rear - the Germans had been reinforced and had counter attacked driving the Russians back killing hundreds of them as they advanced relentlessly. We were panicked and had no idea which way to go. To go east would seem to ally us with the Russians and probably get us killed as well. The decision was made to try to hide and let the Germans go past us, then under cover of dark try to escape to the west or east, whichever from the judging of the battle grounds, to have the closest friendly troops. All thoughts of the hog were put on hold and we hid in houses and cellars. One man even put himself inside the carcass of the hog. We had made a serious mistake in thinking that the Russian attack would succeed. We would have many more weeks and months of cold and hunger to lament this error. The Germans did return, but either they were not fooled by our hiding or perhaps they were just looting the town, in any event they found nearly every one of us - I am sure, but could not prove it, that some men must have escaped them.

I later learned that my former battalion commander, Claude Scales, in another unit had actually made good an escape to the Russian line but that it had done him little good in getting back into allied hands because of the circuitous route he had been sent by the Russians, in returning him to American control. Many POWs had been wounded or killed in this brief liberation episode but were left by the guards who had rounded us up and rapidly moving us out of town to the west. The soldier who had hidden in the hog was found and returned to the column. The Germans who were left in the town had found him when they decided to cook the animal for themselves.

At what they considered a safe distance from the town, we were finally slowed down and had a chance to discuss what each of us had thought had happened in this brief interlude of liberation, anticipation, and recapture. We all agreed that we had been extremely stupid not to run as fast as we could to the east and Russian lines when we had the chance but then we agreed that we had been deluded into thinking that freedom was a sure thing at that point. A general head count, as near as we were able to make it, about 200 of our own POWs had been killed, wounded, or escaped in this all too brief liberation.

After we had thoroughly berated ourselves for stupidity, we turned our attention to the current situation of seeming to have no direction, the cold getting more bitter and no prospect of food. The German guard company seemed to totally blame us for what had happened and were very hostile toward us, acting as though they would welcome any excuse to shoot or manhandle us. There is a psychological term for this called displacement, meaning that they had to blame someone and we were the subordinate and closest to them. We decided among ourselves to do nothing that would provide them any excuse for them to vent their anger on us.

There were rumors that the Russians were breaking through on the front extending from the Baltic Sea south to Hungary. This meant that they were closing in on our column from the north, the south, and the east. The German goal seemed to be to get us out of that zone as fast as possible until they headed us due west toward Poznan in Poland. We made very brief stops for overnight rest and were being pushed forward 15 to 20 miles a day, almost beyond our ability to keep up. Many men dropped out from sheer exhaustion and were shot or shot at, the guards didn't seem to want to even stop long enough to check to see if they were wounded or dead. The guards themselves were also exhausted and were in no mood to waste any energy going back to check a man. At this point, they were not eating any better than we were unless they had been carrying some rations. We noted that there were more frequent stops and we were permitted to dig into snow banks for warmth, largely we felt because the Germans were too exhausted to go on, rather than any concern for our welfare or well-being.

During one of the stops, a most welcomed and lifesaving event occurred. The day had been particularly bitter cold and the snow was getting deeper by the minute because of a blinding blizzard. The guards had found a large dairy cow barn, half of which was empty. The other half had many dairy cows in it. We were permitted to go inside this barn for one of our rare under the shelter experiences, for a warm night's rest. During the night someone had found a way to get into the dairy cow part of the barn without being seen. All night long men were in and out of the cow area drinking all of the milk which the irritated cows would permit them to take. Morning found a large number of satiated prisoners of war and a large number of cows with empty udders. We were glad that this particular morning the guards rousted us out early before anyone found out what we had done. I'm not sure what the consequences might have been.

It was during this phase of the march that alliances between the various groups of POWs began to form. We had decided that only a cooperative effort could help us survive. If one member of a group got a scrap of food, from any source whatsoever, such as a friendly Polish person standing along the line of march or having it thrown to him, he was obligated to share it equally with the others of his group. This also expanded our chance of getting to any source of food. To this point there had been little problem since there was no food. However, the potential for things to get better improved as the Polish people sensed the oncoming defeat of the Germans, making them more amenable to help us. Discussing how we would divide our imaginary food seemed to pass the time and created a kind of optimism which had taken a beating during our brief "liberation." Four days passed, and we were nearly in sight of a Polish town Poznan. Again the rumors were flying. Some said the Russians had already captured Poznan; others said that the German defenses around the town were too great for it to be taken, largely because of its near proximity to Berlin. The latter rumor was correct, the Germans were still in the town, and showed every sign of intending to stay there at all costs.

As we approached Poznan we saw a beautiful city; quaint and peaceful looking, with its old style buildings, built too close together and standing tall, that is, those buildings which were still standing, for the town had been ravaged by bombings and yet still looked majestic. The cobble stone streets were narrow, by our standards, and we were led down what appeared to be alleys with little sub-alleys branching off from them. It was almost claustrophobic just walking down these alleyways. It was also difficult for the guards to keep along-side of us as our long winding column of men snaked its way through the town.

We were admiring the scenery and the gentleness of this town when suddenly I felt a hand grab my arm and pull me into one of the alleyways. The man doing the pulling was quietly saying something in Polish which sounded like "come." The suddenness of this move and the fact that I was well aware that if the guards saw me leave the column, I was as good as dead, sent shudders down my spine. I have to admit I was scared and yet I was fascinated by the thought that I really had little to lose by going with him. A sense of not-too-well-thought-out-adventure took over and I began to run as fast as I could following him into one passage, then a turn to the right led into another passage, then more turns for what seemed an unending period of time during which my apprehension increased. Wild ideas of being taken somewhere to be killed by someone who hated Americans or that this man might be emotionally out of control, thought he had grabbed a German soldier and was seeking revenge for the death of a loved one. Worst of all, if these things did not happen how was I ever going to get back to the column and my buddies without getting myself killed, all of this buzzing through my mind as I proceeded.

All of my worries were for nothing. The man finally arrived at a small house, built in the middle of a row of similar dwellings, much like the houses in an old Sherlock Holmes mystery novel. We entered the front door quickly and on the inside there were several men, women and children all talking excitedly, again causing me apprehension but this was short lived because for the first time in over a month since my capture I smelled the aroma of real honest to God home cooking. I can only say that it was a near spiritual experience and the warmth and love of these people with whom I could only communicate by gesturing, permeated my entire being. They were hurrying around, pushing and pulling on me to get me to sit down. An elderly lady whose face was lined with wrinkles reflecting the misery and despair the Polish people had endured for the past years of occupation, brought a bowl of potato soup, made with real milk and sat it in front of me. Another person thinking I didn't know what to do, picked up a spoon and literally began to feed me. What he didn't know was that I was overwhelmed with the rapid development of events, too much so to really know what I was doing. However, being a fast learner I quickly got the idea and took the spoon and began to feed myself. All the while I was eating, the people in the room stared at me, talked excitedly among themselves in Polish. I regret to this day that I did not know what they were saying but I am sure a lot of it had to do with how I looked, the rapidity with which I was devouring the soup and their awareness that time was running out if they were to get me back to the column of POWs. While I was eating I could feel someone doing something at my back. They were rigging me up with a kind of nap-sack with straps which they put over my arms, and then I could feel the sack getting heavier, still not knowing what they were doing except that they were putting things in the sack. After a few minutes I was again grabbed by the arm, the door opened and we were on the way somewhere. I had correctly guessed that the man was taking me back to the column. At this point, I was praying that he knew what he was doing and that the German guards would not see the return. Running down the back alleys and passages, we finally emerged in an alley through which the column was still passing and I was let in the line at almost the same point from which I had departed. There were gasps from the men in the column but they did a beautiful job of covering my reentry with no one being the wiser. My greatest regret was that I never knew the name of these wonderful, compassionate Polish people, nor did I ever figure out why they picked me - I guess I was just the closest at the time and Divine Guidance was still operating in my behalf.

It wasn't until we had passed through Poznan and had taken a course to the northwest and stopped a couple of miles out of town that I even knew what I had in the sack on my back. Everyone was curious regarding what had happened to me, what I had on my back and what was in the sack. As many men as could, crowded around me at the first break in the march. Bill and Bob were closest to me and were able to form a protective circle around me as I opened the sack. As unfair as it sounds to rule out anyone at this point, you have to remember that we were starving men and at this time manners and logic are not our strong points. Anything could have happened when the men saw food. We excitedly opened the sack to reveal a jar of bloodwurst, a package of cheese, a loaf of bread, a couple of onions, a smoked polish sausage, a piece of head cheese about the size of a square quart bottle and an egg placed in a stiff container so that it would not break. I was both elated and saddened at the sight of all this food. I felt that this must surely be the rations for their family and I was moved by their unselfishness in sharing it with me. I hope that someday in some way I can return this humanitarian gesture, if not to them, to another in as desperate straits as I was.

The sight of the food created a problem. If I shared with all who were immediately present, there would not be enough to do everybody any good. The compromise of the problem was that I divided the food three ways as our Alliance had agreed on previously, then each of us, Bob, Bill and myself could do what he wanted with his share. I then shared some of my part with a Lieutenant, who later turned out to be one of the most selfish men of the entire group and would never share anything he had with anyone. There were many instances of survival need changing personalities or perhaps I should say bringing out the basic negative personality which had been present but well-hidden by the demands of a social structure under civilized conditions.

While getting the food was an exhilarating experience, it was also a sobering one. It was difficult to meet the gaze of the soldier who had not been lucky enough to get even one scrap of the food. Yet at this point no one seemed to harbor ill feelings, I guess it was just the sense of futility of trying to meet the needs of too many with too little to do the job. Another way of looking at it was you win some and you lose some and my number had been called in the lottery.

Continuing with great haste the German guard company led us to the northwest. According to rumor this would take us to the Baltic Sea. What then, we were asking the guards but they just shrugged and sullenly continued to walk. It was very frustrating to me to have been an Operations Officer, whose job had been to map out marches, deal with the logistics of a march and be able to see the destination, to now be in a position of being in a strange country with only the broadest of ideas of where we were or what was ahead or how far we would be going. It was extremely frustrating.

As we moved generally north and edged to the west we came to the Oder River, at its mouth, where it joined the Baltic Sea. Without even a pause we were started across this vast, bleak, barren estuary of frozen water and were quick to realize that we were about to cross a part of the Baltic Sea which was called the Pomeranian Bay. While it was frozen rather solid, there had been some warming trends in the past few weeks weakening the ice and then refreezing had caused it to buckle. We were constantly aware that we were no longer on land and that it was very slippery. We had to constantly watch our footing and our column began to look like a bunch of drunks; falling down, getting up, saying a few curse words, weaving from side to side to avoid a crack in the ice and generally losing the appearance of a column or line of men, but ever going forward.

The first time we heard and felt a gigantic ice boom, (that's where the pressure and the freezing action causes the ice to buckle and raise, sometimes as much as a foot), we were scared out of our wits and we were sure the whole thing would open up and drop us into the sea. The worst that happened was that it threw some of us up into the air causing us to lose our balance and fall. The noise was deafening. This made for a very uneasy crossing of this frozen wasteland, not knowing what might happen next. We were on the ice for the better part of two days, which necessitated sleeping on the ice for one night. This was a nightmare because when you are on the ice, in a prone position, you hear sounds of ice cracking and breaking up for many miles away but have no real idea where the sound is coming from. As you might guess, as tired as we were, we got little sleep that night. Those who did sleep had unbelievable dreams, often waking up screaming that they were drowning.

When we returned to land, we were headed in the direction of Hamburg, Germany. We had no idea why we were going there but as it turned out that was the only direction it was safe for the Germans to go at this point. The Russians had nearly reached the mouth of the Oder River from which we had just come. It was in this general area of Peenemünde that had seen the launching of the V-2 rockets.

Photograph of Infantrymen Passing through Witte, Luxemburg, September 10, 1944
Signal Corps photo 111-SC-194169, image courtesy National Archives (6928082)

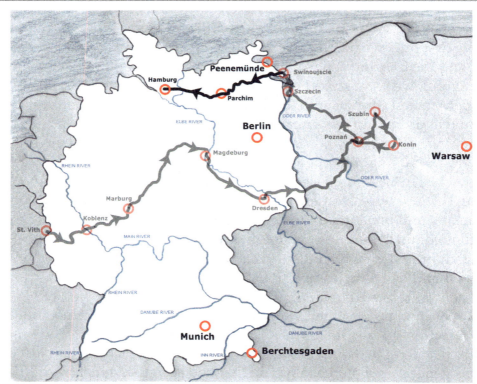

Photograph of Infantrymen moving into the town of Percy, France, August 2, 1944
Signal Corps photo 111-SC-192267-A
Image courtesy National Archives (6928098)

Chapter 6

FRUSTRATION IN HAMBURG: THE CITY AND THE FOOD

In spite of the cold and hunger and the flatness of the terrain there was a sense of relief that the Russian Army was not breathing down our necks as it had been for several days. We heard that they had reached the Oder River but no one was sure at what point on a north-south line this had occurred. We were still being hurried across the country to the west toward Hamburg. Rumors were circulated that the Russians were converging on Berlin and these were easy to believe when you think that the Oder River is a scant 50 miles from Berlin. There was a mounting panic in the German Army and we heard via the German guard grapevine that there were many changes in the German high command, much unrest among the troops; this occurring on all fronts and even that there had been an assassination attempt on Hitler's life by his own staff.

There is no need to deny that all of this unrest in the German high command had an anxiety arousing effect on us as POWs because we had no idea of our status if things should change in the high command. We were undoubtedly a burden on the Army, in spite of the fact that they assumed no responsibility for proper care and feeding. They did have to constantly guard us and use much-needed soldiers to do so. As we discussed this among ourselves we came to the conclusion that there was no place to encamp us, that we were using manpower sorely needed in other areas and that we were an enemy force dangerously close to the very heart of the German nation. In this position they had to consider the possibility that a massive escape or takeover of the German guards would leave us in a position to be a very real threat to their internal security. Thinking along these lines we could see two possibilities for the Germans to consider. One of these was to continue to move us rapidly as possible out of the more metropolitan areas of Hamburg and Berlin. The other possibility was to just eliminate us entirely and we knew they were capable of doing just this based on experience immediately following our capture when many prisoners were machine gunned. It seemed to us that the next few days would be very crucial for them and for us. There were massive air attacks by the Allies on major cities all over Germany and there was particular concentration on communication and transportation centers. This was especially disquieting because Hamburg was known as "the gateway to the world"; having Navy yards, ocean vessels and railroads out in all directions except to the north, of course. It was logically a prime target and it was being hit nearly every night and day by bomber raids. This was just what we needed, more anxiety, for we were soon to enter this city. As we approached Hamburg we could see fires reflected in the sky and could sense the apprehension of the German guards. It was obvious that they knew more of what was happening than we did and perhaps this was a blessing in disguise.

It was getting dark when we entered the city and my impression was that the whole world had gone crazy. There was confusion everywhere. There were soldiers, sailors and civilians going from one place to another without seeming to have any purpose. The city had just gone through another bombing and sirens were screaming, rescue trucks were trying to get through crowds of people, fires lit the horizon and there were many open spots where there used to be a church, a school or even a whole business district. We were herded around much of this confusion and taken as quickly as possible into a Navy yard. I guessed that this was to get us out of the way, also be in position to keep us confined behind high wire fences and to minimize our escape potential; because this was not going to be easy since there were still 2,000 or more of us in this column. Actually there was another purpose which we found it extremely hard to believe. The Navy Command had been advised of our coming and had prepared food for us. We could smell the marvelous aroma of meat and gravy and anything else our imaginations would permit it to be. We were dumbfounded at the prospect of what was just ahead of us, anticipation was out of hand and then our column was stopped just short of, but in view of the tables which contained the large cooking pots, steaming and inviting us. There was a fierce exchange of words between a German SS Army Commander with the rank of Colonel and a Navy Commander. We did not understand the words, but it was apparent that the Navy man was saying yes to something the SS Colonel was saying no. After about 5 minutes of this arguing the SS Colonel gave the order for us to be marched away from the food tables. I cannot find words to describe the frustration, the disappointment and the anger in us at this point. We began to chant "we want food", over and over again, while refusing to move. The German SS Colonel was livid with anger and ordered us to be shot if we continued to refuse to move. He had the guards fire warning shots over our heads, this made us decide to comply. A meal was not worth getting killed for at this late date and in spite of our disappointment and hatred of this man, we obeyed the order to move out - the worst blow of all was that we were walked past the tables holding what would have been our food. Later we learned that the whole episode involved a clash of authority and a jealous rivalry between the Army and the Navy. The Army man had felt that the Navy man was trying to show him up by providing food for us, implying, in his mind, that he could not do his job adequately. At this point in the war, with all fronts beginning to cave in on Hitler, he was replacing generals and staff members almost randomly and in some instances even having commanders that he felt had failed shot. Being aware of the cause of the decision regarding our food, however, did not make us any more forgiving because we, too, were caught in a struggle for our survival.

It was soon made clear that we were going to be taken out of Hamburg as quickly as possible and the only logical direction was the south. Passing through the lesser trafficked areas of the town we could see that almost half of this large city had been devastated by heavy bombs from the Allies. The shipyard and the railroad marshalling yards were hardest hit but with over a million people crowded into this industrial area, the civilian casualties were excessive. It was estimated that 50,000 people had been killed in a single bombing raid and these figures continued to mount as the bombings got more intensive. This very night was a grim reality and gave us first-hand knowledge of the effectiveness of Allied bombing. In spite of all of the confusion, the residents of the city were taking the bombing in stride. I suppose the same thing could have been said of the British during the heavy V-1 and V-2 bombings the Germans had poured on them on a nightly basis.

My feelings as we passed through this devastated city were mixed. I knew that it was necessary to limit the potential of the German War Machine to produce more submarines and war supplies and yet I felt a great sense of loss seeing the destruction of so many ancient buildings, schools, churches and especially the death of innocent people. The tragedy of war is much more than loss of life and hardship, it is the destruction of monuments to the past and a loss of the ties to our heritage. Many of us had grandparents who were born and raised in the very areas that we were seeing reduced to rubble.

As our column snaked its way through the town and the bombings continued, inevitably many POWs were killed and wounded and left behind. Perhaps the wounded ones were lucky because they would be taken to hospitals and possibly be treated in a more civilized manner or at least fed. The rest of us were hurried along and were soon out of Hamburg, again on an unknown course except that it was to the south. It was almost with relief that I watched the lights dim, noticed the confusion lessen and heard the noise of bombs exploding reduce to an almost uncanny quiet.

In resuming the march it was necessary to remember that what had gotten us this far in this entire unreal experience was confidence in our ability to survive because of an inner strength and a belief that it would eventually turn out alright. It is hard to describe the personal mechanisms which account for optimism in the face of such adversity but I soon learned that a sense of humor was vital. This, coupled with a desire to help others who might be hurt or faltering, did wonders to keep the self-pity tendency from dominating the scene. I feel that if a man keeps some control, however little, over his own life and in his own limited space, he has something to hang onto in any circumstance, provided he maintains contact with others in similar circumstance. Practicing this, I am certain, was the very basis of the survival of those of us who did survive.

Rhenania-Ossag Oil Refinery at Harburg, near Hamburg, Germany, was hit by 1,800 tons of bombs dropped by 732 heavy bombers of the US 8th Air Force.
(U.S. Air Force Number A57782AC)
Image courtesy National Archives (NARA 204904567)
342-FH-3A21587-A57782AC

Walter Schmidt, watchman at the Refinery Plant, Hamburg, Germany
June 1945
(U.S. Air Force Number 57767AC)
Image courtesy National Archives (NARA 204904365)
342-FH-3A21477-57767AC

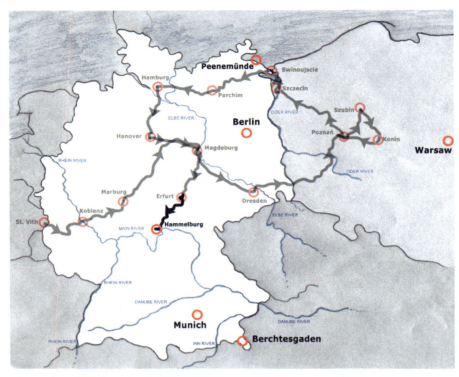

POWs eating on the floor, Stalag IXB, Bad Orb, Germany, April 1945
Signal Corps photo 111-SC-207864, Image courtesy National Archives

Chapter 7

HAMMELBURG AND BRIEF LIBERATION: "TANKS BUT NO TANKS"

The bitterness we felt because of the denial of food at Hamburg was in no way reduced by the rumors that we were heading for a place called Berchtesgaden which the guards said was all the way to the south of Germany in Austria. The prospect of walking a great distance with no more reassurance of food than we had to this point was not a pleasant one and I wondered how many of us would survive such a long distance project - if indeed any of us would. The weather was still bitter cold, our housing was still the great outdoors and our food problems did not seem to have much chance of improving. We were still counting on whatever we could find, anywhere we could find it in order to survive. The great German grass soup, made by putting anything they could find that was green to include grass at times, in a huge pot and boiling it, seemed to be their idea of our steady diet.

There was a monotony to the walking and I found myself singing little songs with each step until I was nearly hoarse. The days passed and the countryside kept falling behind us, with the monotony often being broken by the sound of an overhead artillery shell or V-2 rockets. Strafing of the column got to be a routine thing and with all the energy that we could muster we would move to the right or left out of the line of fire as fast as possible, again fall back in place till the next time.

A new turn of events regarding eating had taken place. When we stopped for the night, the guards would heat up a large pot of water and as I said put everything in sight in the pot, and make a kind of soup which we referred to as "grass soup." It really did have a grassy taste. They would also make up an Ersatz drink, which if nothing else was warm.

One night we were blessed with a chance to sleep inside a very large horse training barn. Except for the walls blocking the wind there was little improvement in the temperature and it stayed down below freezing.

Being normally curious we checked into the various rooms of this very large barn and unbelievably found several barrels of sauerkraut. In spite of its fermented smell, characteristic of sauerkraut, the aroma was magnificent and one at a time we went to the barrel stuffing our mouths with the kraut. It is surprising how quickly filling kraut can be. We felt that either the raw kraut wasn't that great or our stomachs had shrunk. In any event, the barrels of sauerkraut we found were more than enough for the 2,000 of us who were left and although we did not know it at the time, eating no more than we did was a blessing in disguise. The following morning as we lined up to march out of the area nearly every single man had diarrhea and could barely stand up. The guards were impatient and "rousting" us which seemed to do more to cause problems than to solve them. After threatening us and hitting some men with the butts of the rifles, they fired warning shots that got us on the road. The results of the kraut and being rushed were disastrous and men were dropping out to relieve themselves. The guard warned that anyone falling back more than 100 feet would be shot and followed through by shooting 2 men who they considered being too far back. This caused both a tragic and comic reaction. Realizing that we would be shot for falling behind, we would grab our pants and run ahead and hope to finish in time to keep up. The entire scene was ludicrous - rear ends were showing, men running hanging onto their pants and in general the entire scene was chaotic. On the not so comic side, the kraut and the diarrhea working on already depleted physical systems actually killed some of the men who died where they sat. It took nearly two days for us to get back into acceptable shape. Credit to the guards is in order for finally realizing that there was a serious problem and stopping the day's march after four hours.

Continuing our move to the south we were to be treated to two further food experiences. We had noticed large farm complexes with barns and open fields, which looked very much like farms in the United States except for the style of the building. We were told that nobility owned these large farm complexes and that they had slave labor working them. The owners were referred to as Counts and Countesses.

It was one such complex that was to host us one very cold freezing night. We had noticed that the soup had a better taste with a flavor of carrots and turnips. We wondered where, in this war-torn country, in the middle of winter they could get fresh vegetables like this. We were told that they bury the carrots and turnips in the ground in beds several feet across, and two to three feet deep. You could spot these by the mounding up of the ground. Realizing that we were vitamin starved, it seemed reasonable that we should have more of these vegetables for future days since we were in a survival situation and faring quite badly, there was no moral consideration at this point, nor thought that we were stealing. We planned to help ourselves to the carrots and the turnips. After the guards had settled down, we began to mill around in groups as we approached a mound. Several men would block the view with their body, and several others would dig into the mound with hands, sticks, or anything else they could get their hands on. Once the vegetables were exposed, it was a very short time until the bed was empty, the dirt put back and many bulging shirts appearing. Nobody said that digging in frozen ground was easy but all agreed that the effort was worth it as we filled our shirts and trouser legs with carrots and turnips, as our pockets had too many holes in them to hold anything. There was no way we could cook the vegetables and so we just munched on them for days. Just a footnote: The morning following this, as we marched out onto the road, we saw the Countess wildly waving her arms and shouting after the German guards who paid little attention. We asked what was the matter and the guards said, "That crazy woman keeps saying somebody stole her carrots." We were never sure if they knew we had done it or not but it was never brought up again.

Continuing on our way south we were treated to beautiful landscapes, woods, rivers and streams. At one point we were bordering on a woods so thick with overhead foliage that we thought it was the Black Forest until we learned that the Black Forest was further to the west and south. We came across the famous Autobahn which was lined with military vehicles rapidly going about the business of war while we trudged on seemingly without purpose, endlessly day after day.

As with all things time passed, we were moving toward warmer weather. We were headed south, spring was approaching and the miles piled up behind us. There was still hard freeze which worked to our advantage in one instance. The incident involved a dead horse, which had been killed and was freezing as he lay by the side of the road.

The horse had only been killed for a short time and we all saw this as a chance to finally get some substantial food in the form of meat. I could not help but flash back to another exciting time involving a meat carcass while I was still in the United States. I was in the back of an Army 6 by 6 truck, traveling through Mobile, Alabama, in a convoy, where the lead truck was supposed to stop for a relief break every two hours but failed to do so. Being of small bladder, I took the initiative and jumped from the truck, found a service station and then hitchhiked on to Mobile, meeting my outfit. This was considered a punishable offense and in spite of the circumstances, I was punished by being put on Kitchen Police (KP), meaning get up early and go to bed late and do all the dishes, clean pans and help with general preparation of food in any way possible. It was Thanksgiving and we were to have turkeys coming in for this occasion. I was ordered to get rid of a side of beef which was on hand and would spoil because we could not refrigerate it. We were in the middle of a stadium in Mobile, Alabama, surrounded by town and there was no place to bury this beef. I saw a restaurant across the field, and since there was meat rationing, it seemed like a shame to waste this side of beef. I contacted that owner of the restaurant to see if he would want it and he was so delighted with the idea that he gave me and any three of my friends permission to have free meals as many as we would want, at any time of the day or night, for the remaining days we would be in Mobile. Remembering that bonanza, the sight of the horse stirred not only memories but triggered great anticipation of the taste treat in store for us if we could figure out just how to slice the meat. As mentioned before, one of the doctors who was with us had kept a scalpel out of sight of the guards and with this instrument he cut out large hunks of the meat which we would later cut into useable pieces.

That night when we were put into guard position, we were able to take time to slice up any of the pieces of meat into steak size and over a fire which we were allowed to build, roasted the meat. Many men were so hungry they did not wait for this and as a result would tear at the meat, eating it raw. No restaurant ever fixed a steak like it was appreciated more than this horse meat, not too clean, but a very tasty roast. We were quite surprised that the German guards did not give us more of a hassle about having a fire or roasting this meat.

Things were looking better little by little and our hopes began to raise. We desperately needed a boost because we were getting extremely tired and depleted, our bones constantly aching from contact with the frozen ground at night, the loss of weight was extremely serious and our energy levels dropped in proportion to this loss. It was strange how little we ever thought of home or loved ones and how conversation hardly ever went in that direction - survival was tantamount.

After plodding through months of cold, suffering, food deprivation, and lack of vitamins and minerals, our thoughts were concentrated on survival. The unbelievable extent of this preoccupation was pinpointed by an event which took place in a barn on a farm where they utilized Polish men and women as slaves.

We had arrived at this farm after a relatively short march for the day and were pleasantly surprised when we were told for a change that we would be allowed to sleep in the barn. We were resting in the loft when we were approached by a fairly attractive young Polish girl who evidently spoke no English but did communicate quite well with her body language. The way she moved, lifted her skirt and flirted with each man outrageously, made it clear that she had sexual activity on her mind. She went from soldier to soldier flirting and exhibiting herself and was utterly amazed that she got no response or reaction from any of us. Not one man revealed any interest in her. She increased her activity and still got no response. What she did not know was that we were physically depleted, emotionally blunted at this time and possibly somewhat short on hormones or sex generating stimulating food.

The poor girl was so frustrated that she began a tirade in Polish, none of which we understood but it probably was just as well we didn't. She ran out into the barnyard below and began to help with the breeding process which was ongoing and was quite graphic in her moves and activities, often glancing up at us in the loft and reflecting anger and disgust with us.

Chapter 7

The days passed and we had left Hannover, Erfurt and many small villages behind. Rumor came down to us that it wasn't certain that the guards could get us to Berchtesgaden as planned and that a town called Hammelburg was now our destination. Since we were nearly always in the dark regarding location and plans anyway, this news was disquieting until we heard from a recently captured Air Force flier that General Patton was not too far west of this town and moving steadily east in our direction. Anticipation once again. We would be close to allied lines, escape might be possible or we might be liberated. We arrived in Hammelburg late in the day to find that it was, in fact, a prisoner of war camp. In reality it looked more like a fort, with its thick cement walls and cement walled buildings.

We arrived at the gate to the encampment being down to about 1,000 men at this point. As we entered, I once again had the claustrophobic feeling of being closed in which I had experienced in the Oflag in Poland. We were given the usual camp ration of some bread, a small bowl of barley soup and a potato; all poorly seasoned, but nevertheless delicious. The camp looked very little different than the other ones which we had been in; except there was more cement to this one. There was no ceremony about assigning us to beds, we found wooden frames with mattresses filled with straw. There was a potbellied stove in the middle of the room, there was no fire in it, however. Being very tired we quickly bedded down figuring we would explore the camp the next day, since we would be going no place anyway.

To my surprise I heard a familiar and distinctly New York type voice calling my name. It was a voice I had prayed I would hear again, not knowing what had happened to one of my best friends and Army buddies, Captain Edward W. Vitz. I had only experienced this feeling once before, that was when I had found Bob Scheible in another camp.

We spent hours talking about our experiences after the start of the Battle of the Bulge. Ed had been commander of the anti-tank company, which had gotten hit hard and literally destroyed. He, along with the rest of us, had been in full retreat but had had problems getting his vehicles out of the line because of the ice, mud and endless delays. While scouting ahead his jeep hit a land mine and he was thrown out; severely injured his back and rendering him unconscious. He was taken to a German hospital where he recuperated and was then sent to this camp in Hammelburg. He had remained here until the very moment we were talking. We exchanged stories about the long march, finally too exhausted to talk anymore we went to sleep.

It seemed that we had just closed our eyes when the total area exploded into action. Cannons were firing, small arms fire was distinct and the walls were caving in. We were confused, it seemed to be near dawn and we immediately figured that the Germans were finally going to dispose of us. We tried to get out of the locked doors with no success until a shell blew a hole through a wall, which made it simple to get out. We did not go, however; because we had no idea what was going on, on the outside of that wall. All of a sudden it was deadly quiet, we could hear the shuffling of feet, some heavy motors and then the sound of tanks maneuvering. We heard someone shouting to the Germans to come out with their hands over their heads. The voice was in English with a decided American accent and they were using phrases which expressed attitudes toward the German soldiers with which we could all identify quite easily. By some miracle, American soldiers had captured this POW camp and were now about to liberate us. We cheered them as they passed through the gates but they seemed to be all business with no time to waste and told us to hurry and jump on the tanks because we had little time to head west and back to the safety of our own battle line. We learned that they had penetrated 100 miles behind the German lines to get to us. They had fought the whole way there and, as rumor had it, it was all because a Colonel Waters, son-in-law to General Patton, was incarcerated in this particular Hammelburg camp. We never knew for sure whether or not this was true; because events took place so rapidly that we had no time to think of reasons why this was happening. There was not enough room on the tanks for all of the men, so that those of us who could not get on the tanks ran along side of them, taking turns riding and running - we had learned to share. In spite of our depleted condition, we were able to keep up for about a mile headed west from the camp, when we noticed the tanks, one after another, were stopping. They had run out of gasoline. Once again we experienced terror, rage, anger, and frustration. We quickly dismounted and began to turn to the west to no avail. The German tank detachment which had been pursuing our column merely closed in on a hill above us and with a few well aimed shots of armor piercing shells, disabled any tank which even tried to move. Small arms fire discouraged our running any further to the west and I doubt that we could have gone very far under any circumstance because of our depleted physical condition. We were once again rounded up. This time the crews of the tanks were added to our Prisoner of War group and we were put back on the road to Hammelburg. This second aborted liberation was almost more than any of us could stand and our depression was long-lasting, our stamina and faith were being tested beyond belief. Our number had once again gone lower, either because of men being shot, wounded or possibly by some miracle some of them avoiding recapture.

Even though our original number of POWs had decreased because of illness, death from cold, some prisoners being wounded and some escaping, the influx from prisoners from the Hammelburg camp made a sizable column once again. There was a mixed feeling because there were those of us who had already adjusted to the long march concept, newly liberated POWs from Hammelburg who had to get seasoned to the feeling of open air living and finally the angry, newly-captured tank crews who were dismayed at the hand fate had dealt them.

Photo by Joseph A. Bowen of an M4 medium tank of the 47th Tank Bn., 14th Armored Division crashes into the prison compound at Oflag XIII-B, April 6, 1945, two weeks after the failed Task Force Baum raid. The first raid was led by Captain Abe Baum and ordered by General Patton. It had been carried out to retrieve Colonel Waters, son-in-law of General Patton, who was in fact stationed at Stalag XIII-B and the POWs there. Colonel Waters was unfortunately injured during the failed liberation attempt.
Signal Corps photo SC-387230, Image courtesy National Archives

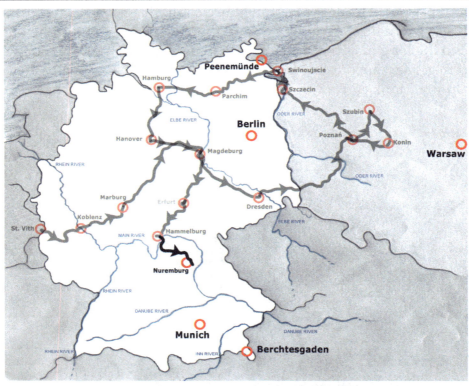

"The first big raid by the 8th Air Force was on a Focke Wulf plant at Marienburg."
Army Air Forces, 1943, Image courtesy National Archives (535972)

Chapter 8

NUREMBERG AND NEAR ANNIHILATION

We learned to accept the frustration, once we had a chance to adjust to the fact that there was nothing we could really do to change what had happened at Hammelburg. The trudging one foot after the other had begun again, with one exception: we were in contact with American soldiers who had very recently been free men and knew what was happening with the war. We eagerly pumped them for news about everything. At first, they were nearly hostile to us, seeming to blame us for what had happened to them and their resulting capture. After all we had a long time, had endured much suffering and had adjusted to the hardships; while they had not yet even accepted their plight, so we did not harbor any ill feelings toward them for their attitudes.

Once they realized that it was a military decision and not we POWs who had caused their capture they were more than willing to loosen up and talk to us. The Allies were on the move, in nearly all areas. The Germans were being routed and things were looking good. General Patton had evidently taken it on himself to try to deepen the penetration into enemy lines, in order to establish a front, very similar to the earlier successful German tactics which had gotten us so badly defeated in the Battle of the Bulge. It was ironic that a fuel problem and not lack of guts or planning caused the defeat of Patton's efforts. The loss of the tanks and the capture of the well trained crews could not help but set the southern American thrust back in terms of time, men and equipment. We often wondered what the top brass who engineered the overall offensive were saying to General Patton at that moment. One thing was for sure, he had shown them that deep penetration of enemy lines was possible and that more planning and cooperation between the Allies might well shorten the war since a weak spot in their defenses had been found.

Information regarding the war in Japan and the situation on the home front was pretty much rumor but optimism ran high. None of us was lucky enough to know any of the newly captured tank men who might have provided us with more specific news about the people in whom we were interested. In spite of our frustrated liberation and only having sketchy information, all of us felt happier and more optimistic just knowing that the war was going well for the Allies and that they were within range. One thought and fear which we all shared was asking ourselves what happens to POWs at the end of a war. We wondered if we would be used as hostages in the negotiations. Would the anger of the German people be taken out on us? Were our very lives in danger? These thoughts were terrifying. We did, however, in our own inimitable way see the brighter side. We reasoned that the German people and soldiers might be more amiable and ingratiating to us, hoping for a more lenient treatment by the Allies in the event of their defeat. We had to wait a good while for answers to these questions and, as it turned out, there was a mixture of reactions on the part of both soldiers and civilians. Some reactions were terrifying to us and almost humorous but all caused much fear and apprehension in us. But wait, I'm getting ahead of myself, specific situations will be brought up as they occur.

Our march seemed to be aimed at heading us east and south in an effort to get us away from the German western front and the Allies and still was consistent with the goal of getting us to Berchtesgaden. Rumor had it that we were headed for Nuremberg which was a very large railroad marshalling center and known to be a major munitions manufacturing area. Both of these pieces of information were good reasons for us not to want to go anywhere near Nuremberg, since the Allies were doing some of their heaviest bombing of the war in the Nuremberg sector. In spite of our fears and apprehension, we were headed straight as an arrow for that town. *En route* nothing much changed except that it was getting warmer with the approaching springtime. The civilians we encountered in our line of march were somewhat more friendly or at least did not go out of their way to be cruel or call us names or spit on us. There were more people willing to offer to trade bread or other edibles for some of the cigarettes or chocolate which we were able to get from our Red Cross packages. The packages were still being divided between 6 and 8 men, in spite of the fact that we were supposed to be given one for each soldier. The German soldiers in charge of distribution were still "losing" many Red Cross boxes. We were getting closer to the Swiss border and it seemed to us that the packages were coming a little more frequently. Our situation had become very confusing and conflicting. On the one hand, things were looking up from a temperature and food point of view but, on the other hand, they were looking very dark regarding our future in Nuremberg with the heavy bombing in that area.

The distance to Nuremberg was relatively short considering the distance we had already covered and soon we were aware of the increasing signs of a very large city ahead of us. For your geographic reference it should be noted that we were coming into the city from the north and west which put us between the city and any incoming bombers which might pass over. We came into visual contact with Nuremberg without any particular incident and were lulled into a sense of anticipation in place of our apprehension. Except for the scars of bombed out buildings, Nuremberg was a beautiful city with the old buildings standing proudly in the background, spoiled only by the tremendous railroad marshalling yard in the foreground. There was much activity and train movement in and around the industrial-type buildings with nothing to suggest that a great war machine was being fed from this very area. Row on row of train tracks could be seen going out in every direction.

While we were admiring the view and anticipating going into the city the guards decided to take a rest stop in a very heavily wooded area just west of town. We were permitted to lie down and rest. We were just beginning to relax when there was the deafening sound of warning sirens. We heard the extremely loud rumble of motors and what we estimated to be hundreds of bombers were droning on in an increasing crescendo to the point that we could hardly hear ourselves talking. The sky was nearly solid with the lead wing of planes going over our heads aiming at the heart of the city. As the planes dropped their bomb load on the city, the city burst into flame and black smoke - it was awesome to watch and terrifying to see the damage done in so short a time. We waited for the all clear to sound, but no - there was no all clear, as another wave of planes came in following the same path and repeated the bombardments. We were amazed to see that anything was still standing when the smoke cleared enough for us to see what had happened. But wait, more thunderous roar of motors and more bombers to repeat the process with one exception: they were now beginning the bomb run on the town earlier, seemingly to try to avoid hitting the populated section and concentrate on the industrial complexes and the railroad marshalling yards. There was only one problem from our point of view: we were in the path of this run and the bombs were falling short and on us in the woods. We were panicked and worst of all there was no place for us to go. The path of the bombers was so wide that running to left or right of the line of approach would only expose us to more direct hits than we thought we could get in the woods. Even here we were wrong: the bombs were making a splinter pile out of the woods and leveling everything in sight. Men were screaming and running in all directions to escape the bombs but to no avail. Those who were hit were in deep shock, one man was running around out of control looking for his arm, which had been blown off. Others were looking for their legs, they seemed driven to find the parts as though they thought they could put them back in place. One of my officers was hobbling around with his right leg blown off at the knee and bleeding in spurts. It was all I could do to get another officer to help me hold him down so that we could put a tourniquet on his leg and stop the spurting blood. He cried pathetically, "Where is my leg, give it back to me." and then he mercifully passed out. The bombs were making craters in the ground as far across as 50 to 75 feet and sometimes 3 to 4 feet deep. Men would disappear in the explosion. We would drag the wounded into these craters for protection from more exploding bombs. As if it wasn't bad enough that the bombs were falling, we were being barraged by parts of machinery from the factories which had been hit - it was a nightmare watching a heavy metal wheel pass over your head or land nearby. Some factories kept blowing up for hours after being hit; we thought they might be ammunition plants, or chemical plants. There was no let up, wave after wave of planes passed over, each dropping its lethal load, circling and heading back to base - unfortunately not all were able to go back. There was no way a sky full of planes could escape the anti-aircraft guns and the flack which the Germans sent up to protect this vital city. Black puffs of smoke and spiraling plane parts were all too common. The bombing continued unmercifully, looking to my left I saw another man hit lying face down on the ground, a piece of metal fragment had cut him up the back as though a knife had been used on him and some part of him was laying actually outside of his body. With Ed's help we were able to open the wound, clean out the part, whatever it was, and put it back inside him. We held him together with a belt. We later learned that he actually lived through this experience with the help of some hospitalization when the raid was over. The bombing continued, we kept seeing trees fall, there was very little if anything left standing as we had crawled into the deeper hole near us. Then Ed let out a yell, looked very odd and dazed and held his hand to his head which was split wide open right down the middle, half of the skull part lying on his shoulder, his brain exposed. We rushed over to him, washed off the brain as well as possible, put his head back into position and actually put a couple of thread sutures in his head, using a needle and some GI thread, which later got infected. In spite of the trauma he did not pass out, although, I feel he was in shock for several days following this incident. Toward evening the bombing stopped. The German guard, what was left of them, evaluated the situation and rounded us up, literally forcing us to run from this area to the southeast. Any man who was ambulatory was helped to move. It was, however, necessary to leave the non-ambulatory men behind. Ed was fairly conscious and with the help of two of us was able to stay with us. He, like myself, feared being put in the hands of German doctors at this point in the war.

Pegnitz River in Nuremberg after bombing, April 1945
Image courtesy National Archives (535562)

Peace Conference of the "Big Three" leaders at Yalta. Left to right: Prime Minister Winston S. Churchill, President Franklin D. Roosevelt, and Premier Josef Stalin. February 1945 just a few months before President Roosevelt died. Signal Corps photo 111-SC-260486 Image courtesy National Archives (531340)

Chapter 9

BERCHTESGADEN IS NOW OUR GOAL

Leaving the open area which a few hours ago had been a woods but was no longer with any trees standing, was to be another anxious time for us. Not only were we pulling, supporting and carrying some of our friends but the German guards had turned very hostile. They herded us toward the road; pushing, prodding and yelling at us. We were faced with a new threat: very angry civilians. The bombing had left them in no mood to tolerate an enemy who was within their reach and they were menacing both in actions and in words. Some were carrying pitchforks and looked fully capable of using them. The guards, in spite of their probable agreement with the crowd, were evidently under order to get us to Berchtesgaden and therefore, had no choice but to protect us.

We moved rapidly to the south leaving the civilians behind. The next couple of weeks were filled with anxiety because there was a war going on now on all fronts and we were being zig-zagged first south and then west and then east to avoid battle fronts. The frequent changes were confusing and not having a map, half of the time we had no idea where we were. There were more frequent stops, giving us time to rest more and do some minor grooming.

Probably the most horrendous event we experienced emotionally during our capture occurred on April 12, 1945. The guards rousted us as usual but seemed somehow more compassionate. It was then they announced, "We are sorry to tell you but your President died." This was a bombshell we had never expected, nor could we fully realize the implications. What would happen now? Would the war effort change? Would the leadership take time and prolong the war? What would the new President be like? How would this affect the German's attitude toward us? Would the death of F.D.R. affect the Allied cooperation? Of course we had no answers to any of these questions but being egocentric human beings our concern was the direct net effect on us in the coming weeks. Panic and fear were combined to give us some very anxious days. Rumors were flying… even the German guards were concerned regarding the net effect on them if the war were to end with a new President in charge.

We didn't have a lot of time to concern ourselves with this problem before another one took its place. We had pretty much shed any superfluous rags or pieces of blanket we had been carrying to keep warm and to cushion us from the hardness of the ground. Carrying any excess weight was just too much effort and drained too much energy; this in light of the fact that it was definitely getting warmer and the need for these items was less.

We noticed that we were beginning to climb gentle slopes in the direction

Chapter 9

of some foothills ahead. What we did not realize was that we were actually going to climb a mountain in the next few days. We were off of the road network and the ground was getting more uneven. Helping the wounded was more difficult and our energy reserves were dangerously close to being exhausted. Thank God that the ascent was slow but even that worked against us because it was spring and it still got much colder as we climbed higher. Prisoners began to drop out of the column, our number from the few hundred who had survived Nuremberg was again dwindling. Thank heavens Ed had gained strength, in spite of the fact that his head had infected along the suture line. He was a hearty man and was carrying his own weight. It was a good thing that he could; because I am sure that we could not have handled any extra load at this point. We were out of contact with any food source and the guards were using some kind of dry ration for themselves. In spite of our miserable situation I have to say that the mountains were breath-taking.

We could see for miles over the tops of lesser peaks and down through valleys. At one point we were actually looking down on German planes as though it were an aerial view. The reason for this situation was that the Allies had total air superiority and these planes were maintaining a hide-and-seek profile so that they would not be shot down, therefore, they followed the lowest valley they could find. The maneuver was not entirely successful, however; because even as we watched, two American fighter planes attacked and shot down a German cargo plane and a Nazi fighter plane, which was apparently the escort. It was as though we were watching a toy situation or a fantasy - everything seemed to be in slow motion. I began to realize that our reactions and feelings were beginning to be dulled by all of the inhumane things we had seen and experienced and by the bloodshed caused by the bombings and strafing which had affected us directly. The worst of all of this was our inability to help to change any of this or help in any way to shorten the war. We were useless to the war effort and we knew it.

Sleeping on the ground at this altitude, with the cold returning, was again taking its toll on our bodies. For weeks we had all experienced increasing pain in our feet, hips and shoulder joints. The cold would penetrate our bodies and a kind of arthritic pain would follow. Our feet were still tender from being frozen back in Poland and the fact that some of our callouses on the big and little toes were as much as a half inch thick began to make walking definitely more painful. This added discomfort and was to persist until we descended the mountain but even then it would not entirely go away.

The only positive things at this point were: one, the German guard attitude was better, two, civilian reaction was kinder and three, the sounds of bombing were getting closer. The Germans called it "the war getting close." The indications are that the war might soon be over. We could only pray that this was true. Once again, however, the question loomed: "What happens to prisoners of war when the war is over?" Are they hostages, are they killed, do they become displacement targets for a country losing a war? It's similar in essence to having no experience with such a contingency or knowing how to face death with no prior experience. One has to wait for what is happening to know the answer and the waiting is hell.

We were now headed west again, seeming to have had to avoid some obstacle or impending attack by some Allied Army, although we were never sure what. There was no way that we could know what the war situation was with regard to which troops were attacking in which zone. The walking had again become mechanical but there was much more contact with the civilian population.

It would seem that some German people felt sorry for us and would actually risk coming up to the column to give us bread or potatoes. Once a man carrying a string of fish passed us and then returned to give the string of fish to us. We were delighted but rather hard put as to what to do with them. That night the guards had built a fire and allowed us to put the fish in an old tin can filled with water and boil it on the fire. In spite of starvation, this turned out to be the worst tasting, most inedible food I have ever tried and nobody was able to swallow any of it. We didn't know if it was a lack of seasoning, the boiling in the old can or just plain spoiled fish but one thing was certain, a starving man will not and I emphasize will **not** eat just anything presented to him in spite of all the popular reference to the fact that he will.

Shortly after this we were aware of being in a more populated area judging from the amount of activity, trucks coming and going and supplies being put in piles along the road. Little did we know these were meant for us - they were the Red Cross packages which had long been promised. The distribution was on the basis of one box per two men, although again I emphasize it was supposed to be one box per man.

The excitement of getting this food was almost too much for us to handle. Dividing the box was somewhat of a problem, since there was only one can of some food and one package of another. The most memorable item to me was the Nestle's chocolate. Once again we had some trading material in the form of cigarettes. Never would anybody trade a morsel of food for any reason. It was difficult to know where to begin eating but the can of beans looked like a good place to start. Experience had shown us that measuring carefully what we were going to eat each time, insured the longest period of time a given amount of food would last. There was also a tendency to prolong the eating process and take very small savory bites. There was powdered milk in the package and I decided to make some chocolate "candy." I made it a purposely slow process. I measured out a couple of spoons of chocolate and mixed it with just a trace of water, making a soft ball. I then rolled this in powdered milk, rolling it out in a wormlike configuration. I then cut this into tiny segments to be savored later at a rate which would be painful to an observer. The whole opening of the packages and the preparation process was like getting ready for and having an old fashioned picnic. The biscuits, jelly, canned potted meat and powdered milk provided us with a balance of food which we desperately needed. I have always been amazed at how we had survived without fruits or vitamins. Perhaps there were more vitamins and minerals in the "grass soup" than we would have suspected from the taste of it. After eating and running through our nearly nightly grooming process, which by now had been more feasible because it was warmer out and we could take off our shirts and pants at times. Each man would help the other pick off the rapidly moving lice in areas inaccessible to him - again the scene would be similar to that seen in a zoo at the monkey compound; except that by now our hair and beards were so long we didn't look much like monkeys. The thing which both amazed and horrified us was to see our bodies (I probably really should say see our bones) and what had occurred over the past months besides the excess growth of beard and hair. We looked like skeletons, with deep sunken eyes, ribs showing no meat, just skin covering the bone, prominent pelvis bones and between them a sunken area making the pubic area a large mound in its own right. You could literally touch your fingers together as you grasped the radius bones at the wrist. The buttocks were caved in and the total appearance was disheartening and grotesque.

On the light side, receiving of the Red Cross packages and subsequent eating of some of the food had a relaxing effect and seemed to make us more able to relate to each other, even to the guards. By this time we had learned some German words and could communicate by supplementing the sentences with gestures and pictures. It was becoming apparent that the guards were more interested in relating to us in a more understanding manner now and we interpreted this to mean they were also concerned as to what would happen when the war was over, particularly if they should lose it. This created a complex interaction which was to become a problem for us some days later. It got to a point where the guards would take time to try to teach us some German words and even show us pictures of a wife, a sweetheart, or children.

We had been walking to the west for several days and noticed that the guards were more uneasy than usual, when two of them walked up to us and offered their rifles to us in a gesture of surrender. We were not sure how to handle this problem since the war was still on, we were in enemy territory, still in uniform however bad it looked, not knowing where we were, nor knowing where the Allies were and not knowing where the nearest fighting German Army was. During training it was said that you would take the rifles and hold the guards captive but not all the guards had done this and as a result we could have been shot on the spot by any guard who did not want to follow this procedure. Our next thought was if we took them captive where would we take them? Next realism, we are enemy soldiers no matter how disheveled we looked, we would be armed and behind enemy lines and, as a result, would be viewed as spies and probably shot on sight by any German troops who might happen by. The truth of this was to become quite apparent just prior to our liberation. After long deliberation we decided that if the war was this close to being over and if the [German] soldiers felt that they had lost it to this extent, our best decision was to remain their prisoner for a while. We felt we had not come all of this way and with all of the suffering, to be shot as spies, the Geneva Convention rules could not save us. The German soldiers were surprised at our decision but seemed to understand our reasoning.

Typical contents of a Red Cross parcel.
Image courtesy special collections branch of the USAF Academy Library

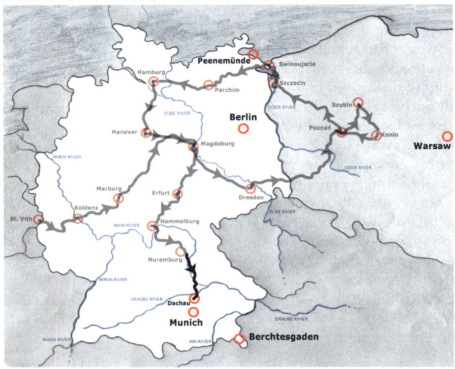

"Pvts. George Cofield and Howard J. Davis guard a newly-constructed bridge site over the Rhine River, built by U.S. Ninth Army Engineers." March 30, 1945.
Signal Corps photo 111-SC-204770, T/5 H. R. Weber and Pfc. Sperry
Image courtesy National Archives

Chapter 10

THE DANUBE AND THE DANUBE

We continued to frequently change directions for no apparent reason and soon came into view of the Danube River. It is a surprisingly large river and was very muddy looking - we were expecting clear water to match our concept of the "Blue Danube" waltz type river. These references were romantic in nature and, as often is true, the romantic idea does not match the reality.

For days we would be plagued with anxiety and indecision on the part of the German guards and the German troops which we had finally encountered. We now knew that our decision to remain prisoners had been a good one. The German Army had not given up in any sense but was in retreat. Their decisions centered around whether or not to blow up bridges as they moved away from the front, wherever at any given moment that might be. We would often be kept back from the bridges and the banks of the river while a decision was being made and then hurried across the river to continue on our way until the next encounter with this winding river, sometimes crossing to the west, sometimes to the south, then sometimes to the east. Bridges on the smaller streams were often blown up just after we had crossed them.

We had been routed around Munich and were headed south where rumor had it that there was a concentration camp ahead of us. We had heard of these camps which were notorious for cruel treatment of the prisoners and rumor had it that the primary group in this camp were of the Jewish faith. This again brought terror to those men in our group who were Jewish but had so far escaped detection. Since our guard unit was Wehrmacht and not SS troops, I doubt that at this point they would have done anything even if they knew a man was Jewish.

We approached a large concentration of buildings inside a high fence. The guards said it was Dachau camp. We walked along the fence to pass the compound. There was no effort to circumvent the main building, and from the road we could see into a window and doorway where there was a large lamp with a very large shade. The guards very quietly said that it was rumored that the shade was made of human skin and that the woman in the house was crazy. The thought that this might be true was enough to make many of us sick but that was only the beginning of the horror of this place. Further along as we passed we could see human bodies piled up as high as 6 feet and covering nearly a quarter of an acre. The stench was unbelievable and many of us threw up what little we had in us. The guards literally ran us on past this obscenity. Never had any of us witnessed such inhumanity and almost immediately we were trying to convince ourselves that we had not seen this ghoulish scene of the past hour. Mercifully the wind changed and we were out of the influence of any physical reminder.

Except for mental blocking to save our sanity, the memory would not go away and served to remind us of how lucky we were not to be in the hands of the SS troops.

For the next few days we encountered the Danube River several more times, always with the feeling that decisions had to be made before continuing with us and determining the direction to be taken.

We continued to wind around the countryside, crossing rivers and climbing and descending hills and small mountains. We passed through many small villages which we could not identify. The names of the towns and the road signs had been taken down so any enemy troops who could get this far could not easily locate themselves on the landscape.

In each village we could hear radios blasting with Hitler's voice shrill and demanding, telling the people to fight to the end to protect their villages, assuring them that he was in charge and would continue to protect Berlin from the enemy. The people's reactions were mixed but the greatest number of them seemed to realize that the end of the war was near. We saw people tear up Hitler's picture and throw it out as we passed so that we would see them do it. We saw other people spit on the picture, tear it down from their wall and stomp on it. Some people, as we passed, handed us food. Some people were very angry, would have no part of being nice to us and would literally try to get at us with threatening gestures and abusive language. People were frantic and the situation was chaotic.

As we approached each village, if it hadn't been so tragic, it would have been comical to see the people of the village trying to defend their town. Even on a wide open space with a road running through it the town's people would pile rocks and logs obviously attempting to stop or impede vehicle and troop movements. What made it grotesque was it was a simple matter to go around such barricades. The population doing all of this was made up of old and feeble men and women, children of age 10 on down and able-bodied women who had been doing men's work in the village and in the fields while their men were at the battle front.

We had run across the older children in various places throughout Germany. They were always dressed in uniforms, generally brown in color and were being groomed to be soldiers. Some of them, especially toward the end of the war, had been armed. These youth camps were similar to our scout camps but with a life and death training program being followed. They openly showed hatred for us whenever we passed anywhere near them. The hate and Aryan philosophy taught to them was certainly effective. There were boys who were evidently graduates of these camps; because we had often seen boys from age 12 on up in actual uniform and in some of the fighting units.

There was evidence that the American command had been alerted to the possible danger to us as POWs with the war seeming to be drawing to a close. This awareness came in the form of leaflets being dropped by Allied planes in cities along our route. We were ordered not to pick them up and were threatened with being shot if we did so. Evidently the civilian population was also alerted. However, there was no way that with that many papers falling from the sky they were not going to be read by somebody. In essence, the leaflets, signed by Dwight Eisenhower, said that under the threat of strong reprisal, no harm should come to any prisoner of war, either in camps or those still marching on the road. It was extremely reassuring to know that someone really knew of our presence and location. We had begun to believe that this was a sure sign that the war was nearly over or at least that the Allies thought that it would soon be over.

The incident of the dropping of the leaflets had particular significance for me, because General Eisenhower was my second cousin (for *updated genealogy* see UPDATED GENEALOGY *on page 97*). His father and my maternal grandfather were brothers. Dwight had spent a good deal of his early years staying with my Uncle Chauncey Eisenhower in Anderson, Indiana and they shared an interest in racing cars. My mother, Birdie Pauline Eisenhower used to go target shooting with Dwight. Thinking about all of this reminded me that my mother had wanted me to go see General Eisenhower when I first went into the army but I had declined, because it seemed too much like brown-nosing. I can't help wondering how different my life would have been if I had followed her advice and gotten on the staff of Dwight Eisenhower. Chances are I wouldn't be writing this book from a prisoner of war point of view.

General Dwight D. Eisenhower gives the order of the day, June 6, 1944
Signal Corps photo
Image courtesy National Archives (531217)

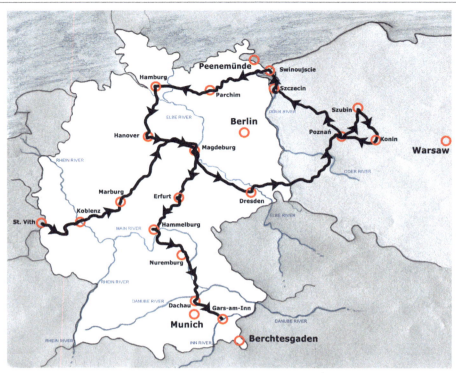

Klosterkirche, Gars-am-Inn
Front of the monastery church at Gars (Mühldorf, Upper Bavaria).
Image courtesy Wikimedia user Siddhartha Finner

Chapter 11

GARS-AM-INN, THE INTERNATIONAL RED CROSS SETTLEMENT

We continued our march to the east moving each day closer to what we had been told was our final destination - Berchtesgaden. Our primary fear was that we would actually get there, they would get us inside the installation and not acknowledge that we were there. According to the guards, the mountain retreat was extremely heavily fortified, was very thick with concrete and much of it was in and below a mountain. The word was that this was an area Hitler had loved and so had built this fortification for himself and his officers in case of a need to retreat. Rumors as to how far away this retreat was and how long it would take to get there were coming through heavy and fast. Even the German guards had reservations about wanting to go inside such a formidable fortification.

We were now into May 1945 and rumor had it that the Allies were closing in on all fronts and that the Russians were already in Berlin. We were not sure whose Army was to our west but from the noise of battle they were only a few miles away. We had just passed through another small town which was fortified in the home-front style already described above. I felt that since there were so few of us guarded by an excessive number of guards, we were no threat to the population and so they could be more curious than angry or aggressive toward us. Except for their loved ones, who might have been hurt or killed, thus making these people angry, these people had not been bombed, nor directly affected by the war at this point. We had passed the town of Mühldorf and immediately ahead of us was another river; this time not the Danube. We were told that it was the Inn River and that we had to cross it. We were being hurried along and told that there was talk of blowing up the bridge, which we were to cross before this occurred. For some reason we were routed upstream away and to our amazement saw a huge sign saying "International Red Cross Settlement, Soldiers Forbidden." Behind this sign was a church which we believed to be Catholic. The church was surrounded by a concrete and stone fence. We were milling around, evidently waiting for the guards to get some idea of instruction as to how to proceed with us. A priest or at least the head of this set up invited us inside the courtyard. After several hours we were again on the way to the river when we heard an explosion at the river. We were told that someone had prematurely blown up the bridge, we could not cross. We were taken back to the church.

The shooting to the west was getting louder and soon a German Captain with about a platoon of men, looking very harassed and moving rapidly, appeared on the horizon; bearing down on our position, evidently wanting to cross the river. The Captain was livid with anger when he found that he could not cross the bridge because it had been blown up.

Photograph of Damaged Bridge Left by Germans Fleeing La Seine, France
August 26, 1944
Signal Corps photo 111-SC-324109
Image courtesy National Archives (593400)

Church of the Assumption of the Virgin Mary at the Gars Abbey
Courtesy Wikimedia user Gliwi, 2012 (CC BY-SA 3.0)

LIBERATION - THANK YOU GOD
& AN UNNAMED CATHOLIC PRIEST

The Captain was in full battle gear brandishing an automatic weapon and looking very cruel. His uniform was dirty and he needed a shave indicating that he had been on the run or retreat in the field for a good length of time. His men looked tired, sad and showed little spirit for battle; showing more a need to rest. The Captain approached us with anger and aggressive shouting, saying in German many things which we did not understand. His actions, body language and his weapon in his hand left little doubt as to what he wanted us to do and was getting us together in the courtyard to achieve. He took the priest aside and talked to him and then in turn had a long discussion with our guard unit who acted completely subservient to him and definitely afraid of him. There was no doubt about his being an SS trooper. At best they had always been cruel and disdainful to us throughout Germany but here it could get worse because in addition to all of this he was nearly defeated, on the run and here we were, ready-made targets for his displaced anger and hate.

After his conferences, which seemed to indicate that no person present was agreeing with him in his position, he strode over to the nearest POW and hit him across the head with his weapon for no apparent reason, just frustration. He then turned to the soldiers in his unit, the one carrying a light machine gun and evidently told him to set it up ready to fire. The priest pleaded with him but he knocked the priest down and proceeded with his preparations. The guard company just stood by seemingly helpless in the face of this man's actions but never taking their eyes off of us. It was clear that he meant us real harm and there was nothing we could do because there were only between 30 and 100 of us against all of these angry, fully armed Germans. At this point, we could fully understand why the Jewish people had not charged against the soldier holding guns on them; it would have just been futile and ended in a slaughter. We had little choice except to conform to his trying to line us up. We could have tried to run for our lives but this would have only shortened the time of his shooting us. We now fully realized that he intended to execute us and we were powerless to help ourselves. We stalled as much as we could pretending to not understand that he was trying to line us up, pretending to turn around when he wanted us the other direction and doing as much as possible to prolong whatever was happening. We would go to the right instead of the left and ask him questions in bad German as though we were really retarded. This only served to anger him more but it was buying time for us. Time for what we really had no idea, all we wanted was some intervention by someone or something and there was nothing in sight. I feel that we all felt that all of the past months of suffering had been in vain and that there was no way we could beat these final odds. There was no Wehrmacht Captain to save us, no Russians to overrun us as they had in Poznan, no General Patton to storm the prison camp as he had in Hammelburg; just a vicious Captain with a soldier setting his sights on us. The guards and Priest were looking on in disbelief as though they expected that at the last minute he would abandon his plan and indicate that it was a cruel joke to play on the American POWs to make them suffer. He gave no such sign and gave an order to the gunner at which point the machine gun was cocked, the waiting was unbearable, everything in us told us to charge the gun, to run, to plead but there was no time for any of this and we felt that it was all over. Each man had in his own way been praying and each of us felt betrayed and abandoned but we had not reckoned with the method of God who had gotten us this far. The Priest suddenly lunged forward knocking the soldier and his gun over and then turned facing the German Captain defiantly. The Captain was so surprised by this action that he just stood motionless in disbelief. At that very moment we could hear the sound of trucks and jeeps and what we thought was a tank. The Captain also heard it and turned rapidly ordering his men to follow him at a full run toward the river but the American jeep with his 50 caliber guns firing was bearing down on the area and the Germans stopped, not daring to fire a shot. The German guard company threw down their rifles, the Captain and his men put their hands on their heads in surrender and the most intense moment of my life was over. There had never been a more welcome sight than this - American soldiers with guns who were not prisoners - liberation - release of extreme anxiety - all at the same time. We all cried, unashamedly and at the same time laughed in joy as we embraced the soldiers who saved us. There was evidently much action in this area of a mop up nature. The rescue outfit didn't want to take any chances with us and quickly ordered us into the 6 by 6 truck and headed west. The Germans were marched out under guard. We were amazed by the speed of which all of this was happening and were extremely sad that we had not had an opportunity to thank the priest for saving us, nor could I ever find a way to find his name or even his denomination - we asked God to thank him for us.

We did not realize it until much later that the guards had gotten us to within 90 miles of the supposed Berchtesgaden destination. If we had actually made it there this story might have had an entirely different ending, I will never know.

The truck took us to an interim camp near Regensburg. The ride there was short and very bumpy, but after all of our hundreds of miles of walking, who was going to complain?

Chapter 12

We were all ecstatic and at the same time numb - emotions were confused - it had all happened so rapidly, and our status had changed so drastically. We had to stop thinking like prisoners and think liberated. It is surprising how, over a period of time of capture, some functions are dulled, others stop working because they are protectively shut off and the net effect becomes one of a dull acceptance with only one goal - get through the situation and survive. This, for those few of us who were left, had done just that. We could only guess at the fate of all of the hundreds of men who had been and were no longer with us at this wonderful moment. We knew where we had left many and what had happened to many others but at this point there was no real enlightenment.

We had envisioned getting to wherever our liberating friends were taking us, getting off the truck and starting to forage for food. This remained a number one priority for us. This was not, however, to be. We arrived at a makeshift compound which already held hundreds of other liberated prisons of war from all sources. We were taken in behind the fenced area and the gate was closed. The feeling was very similar to that experienced when we had been put behind our first enclosure at "Oflag 64" in Poland. We were incensed to think that our own troops were treating us like prisoners. We wanted to be free to move about as we chose even if we didn't go anyplace. Of course, this would have been idiotic on our part at this point in the proceedings, with the war ended and nobody knowing what a defeated civilian population might do to unarmed GI's wandering around the countryside. We had not reasoned out that the liberators had to keep track of us and deliver us somewhere in order to account for us. We were told, not unkindly, but firmly that this arrangement was necessary until transportation back into France could be set up. What made this all the harder was that our liberators did not have enough food to feed us and we had lost our mobility to scrounge for food from the general population, a process with which we had gotten quite proficient by this time.

We were interred in this fashion, sleeping again on the ground for 3 or 4 days and then taken by truck to an airport near Regensburg. I felt good at this point because I had kept a running notebook throughout the period from December 16 to this date, May 2, 1945. It showed names of towns when known, what the buildings looked like, the distances we had covered each day, what we had or did not have to eat. Significant events and in general the attitude of the German people, were important parts of this notebook. The book would have helped keep in perspective what had happened and later helped to locate soldiers who had been killed or wounded in the accounting process. We were kept busy comparing notes with other prisoners who had not been in our group, asking about various friends they may have run across and, in general, getting back to having a life one more time.

The soldiers did manage to bring bread into us, evidently from local sources because I am sure we had no baking facilities this deep in Germany at this time, extending to May 7, 1945. We had survived so many varieties of hardship in the past months, it was mostly our feelings, not our physical conditions which were hurt during the waiting process. The fact of being treated like prisoners by our own soldiers was hard to take.

1,200 U.S. Soldiers escape from POW camp (likely Stalag 12A) at Limburg, Germany March 28, 1945.
Image courtesy National Archives (195464)

*Pfc Joseph Demler of Wisconsin had been captured at the Battle of the Bulge
and was held as a P.O.W. at Stalag XIIA near Limburg, Germany
for approximately three months. Demler is seen here just after liberation,
about May 1945, weighing just 68 pounds.*

*John Mohn had entered the Army at 145 pounds, and at liberation
weighed 65 pounds, much like Joseph Demler in this photograph.*

John Florea/The LIFE Picture Collection/Shutterstock

Chapter 13

LE HAVRE AND CAMP LUCKY STRIKE: AFTERMATH AND REUNION

It was a bright sunny morning when we were told that it was possible to take us to a nearby airport and then subsequently fly us to France for processing, decontamination, briefing and finally feeding. We didn't care, at this point, what the priorities in sequence of events were, we were ecstatic just to be going and above all not having to walk.

Our transportation was to be a stripped down B-25 bomber; a huge plane and very noisy with its gasoline engines roaring in preparation for take-off. We were lined up to get on the plane but discussed that there were an awful lot of us for each plane. The answer was soon apparent, there were no seats. We were just lined up on each side of the aisles, one after the other with feet extended out - it is surprising how many soldiers you can fit in a plane in this manner. Weight limit was no issue, since no soldier weighed very much. We later learned that it took 3 of us to equal the weight of one average man - we were just bone covered by skin, and had no equipment to carry. The realization of the truth of how much weight we had lost was not to be fully revealed until we were stripped down at our destination for examination, showering, delousing and fitting for clothes.

The tension, excitement and apprehension we felt could have been cut with a knife. At this point, we did not want any kind of foul up or delay. We were about to leave this country where we had been abused, starved, frozen, cursed, threatened, killed, wounded, stripped of all dignity and in many ways physically damaged. It is no wonder that each of us in his own way was holding his breath, crossing his fingers and barely saying a word as the plane taxied down the runway. The pilot seemed to take forever to make the turn for the takeoff but as we had learned so many times before, all things come to an end and things do proceed. Waiting is still the hardest part.

The engines revved up louder and finally we began to move, ever increasing speed until we felt a lift-off and then we knew with great relief that we were finally airborne and headed for full realization of our freedom. We talked and laughed and made imaginary plans because we really had no idea what awaited us at the end of this flight. We had full confidence that we would get there and were told that it would be a fairly short flight. The countryside faded away, from time to time we could see a small town and at one point we were told that the very large town below us was Paris and that we were headed for Le Havre on the coast. Paris looked much as it does in all the photos and we were only over it for about 5 minutes. We were not really in much of a sightseeing mood. We were more in a "Let's get there fast (Le Havre) and leave the sights till later" frame of mind.

Chapter 13

As we circled to come in for a landing we could see the city of Le Havre, the coastline and a huge camp-like installation with hundreds of tents and hundreds of soldiers milling around them. After landing we were taken to the camp which we then learned was Camp Lucky Strike. Its sole purpose was to process prisoners of war upon liberation.

There were tents with all kinds of supplies, there were kitchen tents, tents set up like cafeterias, sleeping tent sections and in all it was an American army post set up in France being run very efficiently.

The excitement and anticipation was almost overwhelming. Food at last, a chance to bathe, new clothes, a shave, a haircut, delousing and debriefing, all done in an orderly fashion, with the eating being last. We were stripped down and our clothes piled up and taken away except for our boots. I would not part with mine, they were combat boots and had served me admirably for the past 6 months. In spite of all of the mileage on them, over 1,200 miles, they still had a good sole and besides they were just comfortably broken in.

The next step was to put us in a tent-like shelter and spray us with delousing powder - the lice dropped by the hundreds. The next step was a shower and it was at this point that we finally saw the obscene damage to our bodies - we were hollow cheeked, hollow eyed, rib and pelvis bones were gruesomely protruding and our mid-section was totally concave. This was only preliminary to the shock we received when we were finally permitted to shave. It was unbelievable what the long beards and moustaches had concealed. It was really difficult to remember what we had previously looked like. Our friends sounded right but looked like strangers. There was almost total silence as each of us began to fully realize what the past 5 months had done to us. We were, however, able to comment that even in this state we were better off than the men we had left behind, dead and wounded. We were soon to find out what had happened to many of them.

After shave and shower we were taken to the supply tent and outfitted with complete uniforms. Another shock. "What size for you soldier?" "The regular size for me." "Oh no, it will be some time before you fit that size." It was like when you were a growing kid and the clothes were bought large, "He will grow into them" mom would say, so that for a while you were resentful and looked very uncomfortable in the ill-fitting clothes.

Finally the long awaited, anticipated, prayed for and fantasized food was to be available. We all had definite ideas of what we would "load up" on: steak, chops, potatoes, vegetables, fruit, anything in sight. Medical men had anticipated this possibility and knew that such a choice on our part and eating this much could possibly be harmful to us, and so had a single entrée - spaghetti!! - with a small roll and a beverage, small size. We were furious, we felt betrayed, we felt deprived, how could people in charge not realize that we had to eat to make up for months of little or no food? Sullenly we sat down at the picnic table and began to eat. We had been too long deprived to take a chance on anyone taking this token of a meal from us - we ate. Amazingly after several bites, however, each of us stopped eating, feeling very full and realized that our stomachs had shrunk and would hold very little. Wiser heads had prevailed and saved us from ourselves. Little by little with each meal the amount was increased over the next few days and then we were eating fairly normal meals; although still being very carefully prepared with the type of thing we were permitted to eat.

With our food fantasy finally completed, we were taken in for debriefing where each of us told where we had been to the best of our ability, what our units had been through and who was to be notified that we were alive, even if not too well. During our interview we learned that there had been thousands of prisoners and casualties during the Battle of the Bulge as we learned it had been named, largely because the German penetration had moved the center of Allied lines so far toward Paris creating an actual bulge. We also learned that there had been some marches of prisoners from one point to another with limited scope but nothing to compare to the long-lasting, long-distance march that we had just completed.

We were able to use this information gathered by the debriefing team in order to try to locate friends and fellow soldiers with whom we had lost contact. Bob Scheible, Ed Vitz and Bill Moon and myself had remained together throughout the time in a prison camp to the terminal move to Lucky Strike Camp. All other friends, acquaintances and fellow officers had to be researched. There were some surprises waiting for us. Two fellow officers that we thought had been killed by an extremely large explosion at Nuremberg during the disastrous air raid, showed up in fairly good condition except that they had lost their hearing and were wearing temporary hearing aids.

Charlie, the senior officer of the two, put us in touch with others who had been taken to the same hospital. The soldier who had his insides lying on the ground beside him due to a knife-like incision in his back caused by a bomb fragment, was still in the hospital doing fine. We had to put him back together by washing off what was either a liver or kidney, putting it back in him and then binding him together with his belt. He was the greatest miracle of all the survivors; although Ed with his split head healing well enough that they didn't even hospitalize him, was running a close second.

We began to settle into a routine of sleeping on an actual cot (a real luxury), eating 5 small meals a day (said to be better for us than 3 large meals), bathing and putting on clean clothes - who would have ever thought of all this as being a luxury? We were permitted to write letters and some attempts were made to make phone calls, although overseas communications in an area poorly equipped were not too successful - families would just have to wait to talk to us - suffice it to know we were alive and coming home.

We learned that we were awaiting ocean vessel transportation back to the United States. I had come to Europe aboard the Aquatania, a 4 stack passenger ship converted to transport troops. I wondered what kind of vessel would return us to the states. It turned out to be an older converted transport-passenger ship the SS Le Jeune.

Most of us had prepared for the return home by buying souvenirs in the form of pistols, swords, candy, perfume, beer steins, glassware and a large variety of other objects. There were, however, limits placed on the kind of things permitted and, even though I was allowed to bring a pistol, I was not permitted to bring my beer steins or bullets for my pistol.

Our newly acquired duffel bags were piled at the dock to be taken aboard in large groups. When I retrieved mine I found to my dismay that my much treasured notebook, which I had so meticulously kept, had been stolen from my bag and to this day I have no idea who took it or why; unless they had taken it, had no use for it and disposed of it or perhaps they might write a book like this one someday. The book contained names of towns, as many as I could learn, the miles or kilometers traveled in any given day, where we stopped, when we were attacked by the planes, what we had to eat, names of other soldiers, where they were last seen and what had happened to them. Also included were German attitudes from area to area, detailed descriptions of the landscape, although it is nearly all the same as parts of the United States and our feelings from day to day. It is difficult to remember many of these things in detail and perhaps the truth is that I don't really want to. It is one thing to sit here well-fed working on this book and quite another to imagine the feelings associated with frozen feet, death, dying, starvation, 10 degree weather, losing friends, seeing them die and being hurt.

The trip home was relatively uneventful. The conversations were mostly about what it would be like to see family again, what had happened to friends, had anything changed drastically in 6 months and when were we going to get paid. We were all aware that even though the European war was over, there was still a Japanese-Asian Theater War going on, apparently not that close to being over. Our question was simple - would we be reassigned to other theater operations and, if so, how long would we be permitted to recuperate? No one in charge had an answer to this question and I'm not sure anyone really knew an

Chapter 13

answer.

     We landed in New York and were taken to Camp Kilmer for processing but were first met with our first real meat and potato dinner served cafeteria style. It was like all dreams coming true, almost overwhelming us.

     From New Jersey we went to Camp Atterbury in Indiana close to Indianapolis. I had once owned a grocery store in Indianapolis and prior to going overseas had organized a major parade through the city so that I was very familiar with all important places like the location of the White Castle Hamburger restaurants. The first thing I did on arriving in town from the camp was to go to the nearest White Castle, sit down at the bar and start to order hamburgers with pickle, mustard and onion and a cup of coffee with cream and proceed to fulfill my major fantasy during my incarceration. After 6 of the hamburgers and 5 cups of coffee the owner seeing my skinny body, decided to stop serving me saying they did not want to see me dying in his restaurant with an exploded stomach.

     Reassignment took place at Camp Atterbury and all of us were assigned to hospitals in different locations, depending on what our major problems resulting from the march had been and what was showing up. Many soldiers in spite of the fresh air existence for so long, had developed Tuberculosis and were sent to warm dry climates, sometimes as long as a year. Some men were actually still unable to function and were bed patients in those facilities. Other men developed severe stomach problems and were placed in situations for best care for this condition. Unknown to me, except for excruciating pain in my knees, hips and shoulders, I had developed a form of arthritis and was said to have a stomach distended to 3 times its normal size. I was sent to Camp Blanding, Florida for treatment and rehabilitation. In this process, it is surprising how quickly we lost track of each other. What communication we did have indicated that as quickly as we showed signs of recuperation we were reassigned to functioning units and prepared for duty in the Far East. Fortunately before actual occurrence, the war with Japan was over in August 1945 and we were given the choice of staying in the Army, with a verbal promise of no further overseas duty, or going home. Surprisingly several of my friends chose to stay in the service and were subsequently sent to Korea - I chose to go home.

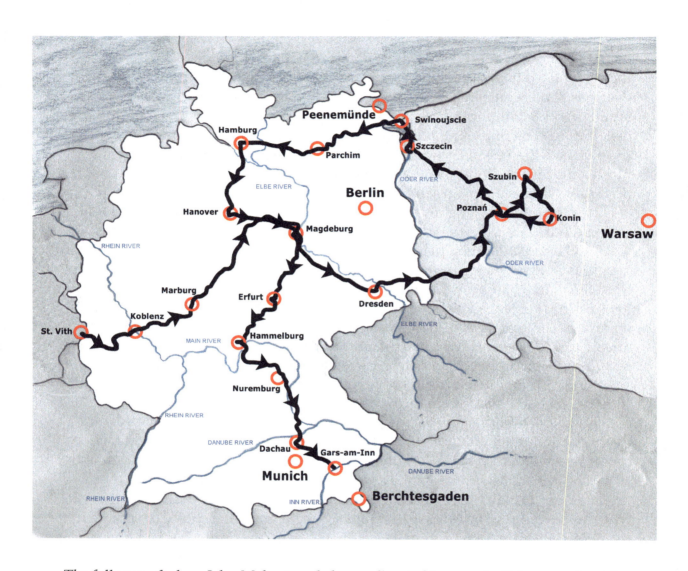

The full map of where John Mohn traveled according to his memoir. It is approximately 1,800 miles traveled, some miles were covered by train rides, but mostly covered on foot. We estimate that John Mohn walked at least 1,200 miles.

AFTER THE WAR

Fate takes many strange turns. Little did I realize the doors which would open as a result of my writing "Forced March." After 50 years, memories dim, except for the traumatic instances incorporated in my book.

I feel there is a completion of the cycle of events and it needs to be a part of this book.

Several months before I completed the book, my wife had heard a radio program in which a couple of ex-prisoners of war were being interviewed. She thought I might be interested so she taped it for me. Being very busy with my clinical practice and trying to write this book, I hadn't played these tapes back. However, after I retired and was doing the final work on the book, I finally played the tape and learned that there was a local organization of POWs. This was a break, because my publisher wanted to know who might be interested in a book such as "Forced March."

I contacted the president of the group and learned that there also was a national organization for POWs called Ex-POWs, which attended need and communications for all POWs from all wars. I joined this group. Routinely the name of a new member is published in the Ex-POW magazine, and my name appeared in the 1993 fall issue.

The next link in the chain was when I got a call from Rick Carnavan from the VA Hospital in Pittsburgh, Pennsylvania, telling me that he had seen my name in the Ex-POW magazine. He said that the VA Hospital there sponsored a group of former members of the 106th Division and some former POWs and that he would like for me to attend their next meeting, which I did. These meetings are on the third Thursday of every month. While there I learned that there is a national organization of former 106th Division members which I then joined. This group also publishes the names and addresses of members.

The important aspect of this series of events is that I have now heard from and located many former army friends who after 50 years have made it a point to make contact. Most gratifying of all, my communications sergeant who I thought was dead all of these years, called me two weeks ago being very much alive.

Some of the names I have run across and made contact with are Anthony Marino, Colonel William P. Moon, Colonel Joseph Mathews, Jr., Major Edward W. Vitz, Sergeant Jerry Alexis, and (Major or Captain) Michael N. Thome. These are just a few of the potential contacts to date.

Postscript

Anyone interested in contacting an old army buddy, friend or acquaintance can find information here:

106th Infantry Division Association
Web: **www.106thinfdivassn.org**

American Ex-Prisoners of War
National Headquarters
3201 East Pioneer Parkway #40
Arlington, TX 76010-5396
817-649-2979
Web: **www.axpow.org**

Updated Genealogy

(From page 75)

Because the Eisenhauer families kept in touch through the years, it seemed to my Dad that the relationship was closer. The spelling of the name changed as each Eisenhauer branch moved to a different area. After years of research, it was found that Dwight David Eisenhower and Birdie Pauline Isenhour Mohn were 4th cousins. It was Dwight's great-great-grandfather, Peter Eisenhauer, and Birdie Pauline and her brother Chauncey Isenhour's great-great-grandfather, Johannes Eisenhauer who were brothers. So, John J. Mohn, son of Birdie Pauline, was a 4th cousin, once removed to Dwight D. Eisenhower.

- *Genealogy done by Debora Mohn Altimus.*

John J. Mohn Biography

by daughter, Debora Mohn Altimus

JOHN J. MOHN 1919 – 2005

I start with my Dad's obituary.

"1/27/05 NORTH LIMA - John J. Mohn, 85, of 12691 South Ave. died Tuesday morning January 25, 2005 at his residence following an extended illness. He was born on June 17, 1919, in Akron, Ohio the son of John A. and Birdie Pauline (Isenhour) Mohn. He moved to the [Youngstown, Ohio] area in 1956.

Mr. Mohn was a clinical psychologist who taught at several universities including Youngstown State University (Youngstown, Ohio) and Mount Union College (Alliance, Ohio). He was also Guidance Director for Poland Schools (Poland, Ohio). He retired in 1990 after 40 years working in his field. He had received his undergraduate degree from Akron University (Akron, Ohio) and his Masters Degree from Case Western Reserve University (Cleveland, Ohio). He was a Purple Heart Recipient having served in World War II as a U.S. Army Major in the 106th Infantry Division. He was captured in Belgium at the Battle of the Bulge and was a P.O.W. for five months before he was liberated by U.S. Forces at Gars Inn in Germany. He was 1 of 100 who survived out of a total of 7,000 who were captured.

Services will be held at 1 p.m. Friday at the Seederly-Mong & Beck Funeral Home in North Lima with Rev. Barry Stirbens officiating. A full Military Service will be conducted by the American Legion Benjamin Post 290 of Columbiana. Burial will be in the North Lima Cemetery. Friends may call from 7 to 9 p.m. Thursday at the Seederly-Mong & Beck Funeral Home in North Lima."

Biography of John J. Mohn

This was my Dad. Summed up in a few paragraphs but he was so much more than this. He was caring, loving, generous and funny. He was a very intelligent man. He was protective of those he loved. He became a Psychologist to help those in need. To see how my dad, John J. Mohn lived his life, you must first see what kind of a family he came from. It was a very adventurous family.

His grandparents, Adolph and Anna (Boehme) Mohn were from the Dresden area of Germany. They had come over to America in August of 1882 with their young son, Oscar, to live near Adolph's older brother, Ernst Mohn, and his family. From Dresden, The Mohn family traveled 295 miles to get to a port in Bremen, Germany where they boarded the steamship "Hermann." Adolf, Anna and Oscar had quite an adventure coming into the United States. Ernst had come over 9 years earlier, in 1873. I can only imagine that he might have written a letter telling his younger brother Adolph to come to America for the opportunity of a lifetime.

Nearing the end of their journey, when they were close to Baltimore, Maryland's port, the ship had wrecked on the rocks, so all aboard had to wait to be rescued by another ship. Not only that, when the rescue ship finally took them into the Baltimore Port, all passengers were quarantined because of an outbreak of the measles. So, Adolph, Anna and two year old Oscar Mohn were kept in Baltimore for another 2 to 3 weeks before they were allowed to travel on to Akron, Ohio.

Anna (Boehme) Mohn c.1890s Oscar & Jack Mohn c.1886
Altimus Family Collection

Biography of John J. Mohn

In Akron, Adolph, Anna and Oscar settled into a home on Yale Street. Adolph worked at the J. F. Seiberling Co. rubber factory and Anna sold eggs and did laundry for others to help with the bills.

The following year, John "Jack" A. Mohn was born in Akron, Ohio in 1883. This was John J. Mohn's father and my grandfather. He was the first generation of our Mohn family to be born in the United States of America. Disaster hit after only six years of being in this new country. Adolph died of cancer, leaving Anna to raise their two children alone. The J. F. Seiberling Co. paid for his funeral and burial expenses.

Thank goodness that Anna's father William Boehme, had come over from Germany soon after Anna & Adolph did. He also lived in Akron, right next door and I bet that he helped in raising the two boys.

At age 5, Jack Mohn went to kindergarten and he had a tough time. Not only had his father just died, he didn't know any English. His family spoke only German at home. So he learned how to speak English in his kindergarten class. He told me there was a lot of pointing and hand gestures by the children and the teacher to get the meaning across to him.

When Jack was an adult, he traveled from the Akron area and went out west to explore. He ended up living in Wisconsin and worked as a bartender and waiter at Lawrence's Lunchroom in Milwaukee by 1904.

Jack Mohn (3rd from the left) bartender at Lawrence's Lunchroom
Milwaukee, Wisconsin, 1904
Altimus Family Collection

Jack Mohn & possibly his cousin Fred Mohn at Balanced Rock in Mushroom Park, west of the Garden of the Gods near Manitou Springs, Colorado, c. 1903. Altimus Family Collection.

Jack Mohn driving a car in 1905. Altimus Family Collection.

Jack's older brother Oscar, met a girl named Sarah, from Wisconsin. In 1908, Oscar and Sarah were married in Akron, Ohio and stayed in the Akron area. In 1916, Jack Mohn met Birdie Pauline Isenhour (known as Pauline) who lived in Indiana but was traveling in Wisconsin, selling magazines. She was a 4th cousin to Dwight D. Eisenhower. Jack and Pauline fell in love and married in Columbus, Ohio in 1917. They moved back to Jack's birthplace of Akron, Ohio to start a new chapter in their lives.

Birdie Pauline Isenhour & John "Jack" Adolph Mohn, c. 1903 Altimus Family Collection

Biography of John J. Mohn

Pauline Isenhour, having been married twice before, had her son Earl or daughter Ella living with Jack and her, at any given time and Jack Mohn, didn't mind at all. On June 17, 1919, Jack and Pauline's first son, John J. Mohn, was born at 733 Schell Street, Akron, Ohio; just after WWI fighting had come to an end.

Jack Mohn & Pauline Mohn
with son, John J. Mohn, 1919
Altimus Family Collection

In 1920 Jack started a career by becoming an inspector for Underwriters Laboratories. A year later, Jack and Pauline had a second son Robert. They nicknamed him "Buster" or "Bus," for short. John and Bus went to Grace elementary school in Akron, where their father had gone before them.

Childhood illnesses plagued the family in 1928 to the point where John and his brother could not go to school for a whole year because of quarantines placed on the home.

Left: John J. Mohn, 10 years old
Right: Robert "Bus" Mohn,
9 years old, 1929
Altimus Family Collection

Biography of John J. Mohn

John J. Mohn missed all of 4th grade but was so intelligent that when he was well again, he caught up on his studies of 4th grade and 5th grade at the same time in 1929. He was sickly but at the same time he was strong in spirit and got through the measles, mumps, rubella, chicken pox, scarlet fever, and even accidentally falling into a vat of chemicals with his brother Bus, resulting in both of them being in a coma for a few days. I believe that this was the start of John's "Mind over Matter" belief. Later, this would carry him through the war in the toughest of times.

After all the childhood illnesses were done and things were back to normal, the Mohn family could travel all over the place. They would camp in the deep woods of Canada; go to the summits of mountains in Pennsylvania; visit Washington D.C., go see family in Indiana or just travel somewhere new for an adventure. Pauline was the instigator of impromptu traveling. Everyone loved to go.

About 1934, while living in Akron, his parents decided to buy a house, out in the Lakes Region of Coventry, Ohio. There was enough land for the family to start building another house close to the first house on their new property with the intent of connecting the two into one home. So every weekend, the Mohn family would go and complete more work before moving out there permanently. It looked like a Bavarian style home with the dark beams showing through the beige stucco on the outside.

When it was finished, the local people called it "The Castle" but the Mohn family just called it "the lakes house." It was large enough for their family to visit.

The Lakes House, 298 Olden Ave., Copley, Ohio 1939, Altimus Family Collection

Biography of John J. Mohn

John and Bus did not join Jack, Pauline and now sister Phyllis moving into "the lakes house." They were still going to West High School in Akron and wanted to finish there. During the week, John and Bus stayed in the house that their parents still owned in Akron. Jack and Pauline had segmented this house into apartments and rented them out to people. There was a maid at the house and she cooked for the boys during the week. And on the weekends, the boys went to back to "the lakes house" to be with their family.

Being in the country near a lake was the best thing to happen to John and his brother Bus. They enjoyed picnics, hiking, swimming, boating, rowing, bonfires on the beach, playing badminton and croquet. Swimming and boating strengthened them both and they were finally healthy for their adult life.

Left: John and Bus in the lake. Right: Jack and son John, going out in the boat. Coventry, Ohio, 1937. Altimus Family Collection

For some reason, after graduating High School in 1937, John decided he was going to walk to Texas. He hopped trains, talked with hobos and walked 100 miles going down to Texas and back to Akron. Oddly, this would be a sampling of what he would be doing as a prisoner of war 7 years later in Germany.

John J. Mohn enrolled at the University of Akron, not knowing what vocation he would choose. Among the classes he took was ROTC. ROTC stands for Reserve Officers' Training Corps. This class trains officers for all the armed forces in college with the expectation that one would be placed higher up in rank when joining any of the armed forces.

John completed the ROTC training and when he enlisted in the army in 1941, somehow his ROTC experience was not recorded, (he says he forgot to say something) so he was put into the army as a Private. I think divine intervention was at work even at this early point of the war for John.

Biography of John J. Mohn

We've all come to the conclusion that if he would have gone into WWII with a higher rank, that would have put him into a situation where he would have probably died early on in the war. And this situation illustrates another one of my Dad's sayings "Everything for a reason." He taught me this and I live by it every day.

After joining the Army, he made his way up the ranks including going to Officer's training school in Georgia. John had army training all over the US. For more about John's stateside training, see the Introduction, "Before the Bulge" at the front of this book.

A very young and eager John J. Mohn at 23 years of age at Officer's Training School. On Back: "Don't you dare keep this fellow in Georgia."

His father, Jack Mohn; Helen (wife of Robert "Bus"), John & first wife Katie, 1942. Altimus Family Collection

John married his girlfriend Katie in 1941 and in that same year, John's mother, Pauline, died in August. Pauline never saw her sons being shipped off to Europe nor did she have to worry when Bus was injured flying over Italy in the fall of 1944 or when John went missing in December for 5 months. John said that he thought about her and often felt her watching over him. John also thought about his brother Bus and what he was going through during this war. Several letters were sent to Bus before John became a prisoner of war.

His family would visit from time to time wherever he was.

1942: John and his sister Phyllis; John & his Aunt Clara Isenhour;
Sister-in-law Helen, John & sister Ella.
Altimus Family Collection.

Robert F. "Bus" Mohn (standing second from left)
95th Bombing Group of the 415th Bombing Squad, US Army Air Force, WWII
Photos in the Keith Mohn Collection

Biography of John J. Mohn

Here's one of the V-mail letters John sent to his brother Robert F. "Bus" Mohn, on Dec. 11, 1944. This was right before John was captured at the Battle of the Bulge.

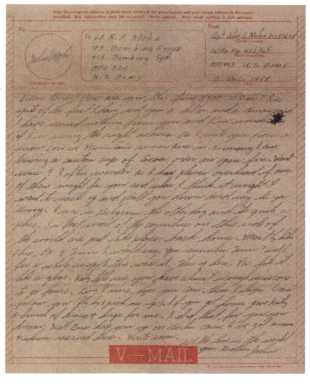

"Dear Bus, How are you this fine 0500 11 Dec? In spite of the fact I have sent you a letter and a xmas card I have received nothing from you and I'm wondering if I'm using the right address. As I write to you from a snow covered mountain somewhere in Germany I am brewing a canteen cup of Cocoa over an open fire. Want some? I often wonder as I hear planes overhead if one of them might be you and when I think it might I want to reach up and pull you down and say hi ya Bussy. I was in Belgium the other day and it's quite a place. In fact most of the countries on this side of the world are just like places back home. Mostly like Ohio, Pa & Tenn. I would say. You remember Tenn? Well for a while in spots this was it. Then up here Pa. fits it like a glove. Katy tells me you have almost enough missions to go home. Boy I sure hope you can then I hope I can follow you (fly by and pick me up). If you get home give Katy a bunch of kisses & hugs for me. I did that for you, you know. Well Bus keep your eye on Berlin 'cause I've got a room & shower reserved there. Write soon. All the love in the world, your brother John."

When John was captured at the Battle of the Bulge, and he was forced to march, he knew his brother was in the 95th Bombing Group of the 415th Bombing Squad of the Army, so he figured that Bus was probably flying overhead while John was marching as a POW down below. In reality, his brother Bus was indeed flying overhead and periodically would drop care packages at various points over Germany in hope that John would somehow find them. The packages consisted of food, clothing (socks, gloves, scarves) and anything else that might help John. But John never did find any of the packages.

Biography of John J. Mohn

After the war was over, he came home to his family who thought he was dead during those five months. Adjustment was difficult at first. He tried to get back to normal. John went back to working several different jobs at the same time and went back to Akron University, but this time for a degree in Psychology because of his POW experience. John and his wife divorced a while later. He then went on to get his Masters degree in Psychology up at Case Western Reserve in Cleveland, Ohio.

In 1954 my Dad, John Mohn, married a second time, to Cheri Roberts, also from Akron, Ohio. When I was born, a few years later, they had bought their first house in Austintown, Ohio.

Dad (John), Mom (Cheri) & me (Deb) 1958. Altimus Family Collection.

My Dad had a job working at Fran Scott, a job recruitment business, not in his field of Psychology but it paid the bills. Mom was an artist, just getting started in the art field and was also going to Youngstown State University. Finally Dad got a break a couple of years later and started working as a Psychologist with the state of Ohio. He tested clients for the State of Ohio; he also taught for Akron University (Akron, Ohio) and Mt. Union (Alliance Ohio); had a private practice; worked with children at the School for Mental Retardation; was a counselor at Poland Seminary High School (Poland, Ohio); worked at the Cleveland Hearing and Speech Center and with Youngstown's Children's Services. He was always energetic and he could definitely multi-task. He only needed 4 or 5 hours of sleep a night to function.

Biography of John J. Mohn

Between all our schedules, we were always going somewhere. I enjoyed it and I know my parents did too.

Mom started Cheri Mohn School of Arts, in an old mansion in Youngstown, Ohio that my parents bought and converted. We lived on the first floor and the third floor was rented out to a family who needed a place to live. But the second floor rooms were made into art classrooms. My dad was handy at building things so up went walls to make an office and old doors were transformed into art tables for mom's students. A lot of hard work went into opening this school. They had art shows on the lawn and a lot of students, parents, teachers and people from the community came to see all that they created.

Left, 1962 Mom opens Cheri Mohn School of Arts. Dad (John) is on the stool in red shirt.
Right, 1963 Student Art Show at 242 Broadway, Youngstown, OH.
Altimus Family Collection

In 1964 my Dad got sick and nearly died. He had ulcers that went into peritonitis (perforation of the stomach lining). I believe this was a result from the war and the terrible eating conditions he encountered as a POW. He usually handled them well, but this one time, he collapsed onto the porch and told me to run and get mom. He ended up in the hospital, having emergency surgery with only a 40 percent chance of survival. But something in my Dad kicked in gear and he healed very quickly. So quickly in fact that when they were ready to remove the staples and stitches, his skin had already healed over them. The ulcers continued to plague him off and on for the next 40 years, until doctors found out that they could be cured by taking antibiotics in the 1980s.

Biography of John J. Mohn

After Dad got out of the hospital, we simplified our life and moved to a townhouse in Boardman, Ohio. This way, my Dad could heal without having to worry about fixing things in the old mansion/art school. It was after my Dad was fully healed and could work full time again that things got back to normal.

Dad never talked much about his life in the Army unless we asked him. It wasn't that he didn't want to talk about his experiences, it was just that he never carried around bad feelings, could compartmentalize to keep the bad in the past and keep all the good that came out of it.

Our favorite vacations were any ocean beach. It didn't matter whether it was the east coast, west coast or gulf coast.

Mom, Dad and I on our summer vacations at the beach, 1966. It is apparent that my Dad stayed very thin after the war, Altimus Family Collection

We also would go up into the mountains of different states, over to New England, out west to see different things like the Buffalo Ranch in Oklahoma, to California to see snow on mountains in the summer, the gulf coast of Texas and down to Florida many times. By 1979, Dad, Mom and I had traveled through 43 of the 50 states, often going out of the way to drive over to the corner of a state, just to say we were in it. We had such fun times. I loved our adventures. Sometimes we would go on vacation with my Uncle Bus and his family.

Bus, John, and Deb Mohn; Helen and Cheri Mohn;
Keith and Steven Mohn
1967, New Mexico
Keith Mohn Collection

Biography of John J. Mohn

One time, in 1963 while going out to visit my Dad's older half-brother Earl in California, we went out of our way to visit a ghost town in Mogollon (pronounced 'Muggy-yon'), New Mexico that Youngstown artists were saying was a fantastic place with gorgeous landscapes to paint. It was a true artist's haven. No electricity or running water, so it was pretty rustic. There were only 15 people who lived there year round. So we drove out there to see what all the fuss was about. My Mom and Dad fell in love with Mogollon, the mountains, the gorgeous landscapes, the people and ended up buying the old abandoned theater.

John, Cheri and Deb Mohn, 1966
We owned this theater in the ghost town,
Mogollon, New Mexico. Altimus Family Collection.

I can still see my Dad, with his cowboy boots climbing the ladder up onto the tin roof to patch about a hundred bullet holes, where the patrons in the early 1900s watching the shows and silent movies would shoot their guns into the air when they liked the performance! It took him many days on the tin roof, tarring each hole so we didn't have any more leaks in the theater. My Dad also built an apartment for us on the stage in our third summer there, so when we would vacation out there we had a place to stay.

In 1967, the ghost town finally got electricity. So that year the Ol' Mogollon Theatre was updated with electric lights and outlets with the help of one of the local guys. We also bought a little refrigerator and tiny stove so we could have cold milk and hot food. We could see at night with the electric lamps. We brought our electric blankets from home because even though it was summer, it was so cold at night until the sun came up in the late morning over the mountain top. It was wonderful to be there each summer.

1967 our "Stage Apartment" right after we got electricity in the ghost town & hooked up to the Ol' Mogollon Theatre. Mom (Cheri Mohn) sitting at the table. Altimus Family Collection.

My parents worked hard for three years fixing everything until events happened and we weren't able to open the theater and the Ol' Mogollon Theatre had to be sold. Mom was very sad but it was nice that the new owners would send progress photos of how they were doing. So we could enjoy it vicariously. This was my Dad, always going into a situation without knowing what was ahead but making the best of it when he got there.

After living in the townhouse, we moved further south to North Lima, Ohio. Out in the country, lots of fresh air and the beautiful land regenerated us all. It had a small pond that we could fish in, swim in and row around in a boat.

Biography of John J. Mohn

1972 Back yard of our North Lima house & view of the lake, Altimus Family Collection

Mom had the sun porch as her studio. And later Mom and Dad created another art school in the lower level of our house. Dad still worked as a psychologist and mom had her studio, art school and framing shop. Life was good. It was funny to see, when my Dad came home from working, he'd just hop on the tractor and cut our six acres of grass, in his suit. We were city people living in the country. We adjusted after a bit.

1969 Here's my Dad showing his brother Bus, his "new" tractor. It was a renovated 1922 International Harvester, Altimus Family Collection

Biography of John J. Mohn

Over the years Dad taught me many things, like how to play chess; how to cook his few specialty dishes (yes he cooked!); play badminton; to climb mountains; to swim and dive; to be street-smart in the city. But in 1969, my father told me the most amazing thing. The former president of the United States, Dwight D. Eisenhower, who had just died, was his cousin and that my Dad's mother, Birdie Pauline (Isenhour) Mohn, knew him and their Eisenhower and Isenhour families visited each other up until they were well into their twenties. That started my love of genealogy. And Aunt Helen Mohn who saved all the old photos, helped it along.

As time went on, I married Rick, my high school sweetheart and moved out of the house to start my own family.

Dad was diagnosed with emphysema in 1985, but he still made the most of every moment. He and my Mom came to visit us wherever we were living at the time and they took vacations to the beach whenever they could. It was about this time he finished writing his book. He had worked on it in between his jobs and "normal" daily life. My Dad could multi-task like no other person!

Mom painted, taught art and then opened up an antique shop. Even with emphysema, Dad helped with the antique shop and around the house. He still practiced as a Clinical Psychologist until about 1990.

Thanksgiving 1999 Dad, Mom, Marc, Mandy, Rick and I (Deb).
Altimus Family Collection

After he retired, Dad decided to take up painting. My mom tried to get him to paint many years before, but only now was he ready. He loved barns so that's all he would draw or paint! His other hobbies were collecting and fixing old clocks; refinishing wooden things like tables, shelves and chairs.

It took 20 years for emphysema to take his life. And the last thing he said to me was "I love you Dee." He died the next morning. That was in January of 2005. Five months later, my Mom died of cancer. I miss them very much.

My Dad was an amazing man. I loved him with all my heart. And I know that he lived the fullest life that any man could. I'm so glad that he lived through the war and I'm so glad he loved us enough to share his life stories and lessons with us. And now with the help of my husband Rick and daughter Mandy, we will pass on his words of wisdom to the rest of you.

Courtesy of Mike Bardin at the Ohio Society of Military History Museum,
formerly in Massillon, Ohio.
Now housed within Military Aviation Preservation Society (MAPS) Museum
2260 International Pkwy, North Canton, Ohio 44720

Debora Mohn Altimus

Debora is the only child of John J. and Cheri Mohn. She is a graphic artist, gardener, genealogist, researcher and now publisher. Deb volunteers at the Massillon Museum gardening and assisting in the archives. She organizes art shows, exhibiting her late mother's artwork. She has been collecting, scanning and saving all the family photos in all branches of her family tree. Debora's Aunt Helen Mohn (wife of Robert F. "Bus" Mohn) had started Deb down the path by giving her an album of preserved historic Mohn, Boehme and Isenhour family photos. Among these, were precious photos of Deb's father while he was in the military during WWII. Many of these photos are shared with the readers in this book.

Debora is married to her high school sweetheart, Rick Altimus, and has two adult children, Mandy and Marc. With a great amount of help from her daughter, Mandy and husband, Rick, they have been making Debora's father's book a reality. Mandy and Rick have extensive historic knowledge which has come in handy in presenting facts leading up to John's forced march as a POW.

Rick Altimus

Rick Altimus graduated from South Range High School, North Lima, Ohio, where he met his wife, Debora Mohn Altimus. Rick graduated from the University of Akron with a Bachelor of Science in Electronic Technology. He currently works as a software engineer and software architect. Rick has always had a love for history. He spent many hours with John Mohn and became familiar with his POW story. Rick helped to narrate his daughter's 2003 documentary about John Mohn's POW experience.

Edward P. McHugh

Edward McHugh was a veteran of the U. S. Army who served in an intelligence unit in Germany during the Cold War. He was a longtime student of the Battle of the Bulge and the last months of World War II in Europe and visited most of the sites mentioned in Major Mohn's story. Edward passed away in 2018.

Mandy Altimus Stahl

Mandy Altimus Stahl graduated from Kent State University with a BA in history, *summa cum laude* with honors. She works as the Archivist for the Massillon Museum. Stahl oversees the care and access to the photographs, rare books, documents, and institutional items in the archives.

Stahl has produced documentary film works such as *John Mohn: P.O.W. in Question* (2003), *Massillon in the Great War: Voices from the Archives* (2017), *The Legacy of Steel* (2004), *The Greatest Generation* (2008), and *Faces of Rural America* (2011). She was the 2016 plenary speaker for the Society of Ohio Archivists, and in 2015 appeared on Travel Channel's Mysteries at the Museum, retelling the tale of Jacob Coxey's 1894 protest march.

Her book, *Early Massillon and Lost Kendal*, was published by Arcadia Publishing in 2017. Stahl serves on the Massillon Historic Preservation Commission, as secretary of the Spring Hill Historic Home board of trustees, and as treasurer for the Charity School of Kendal Foundation. In 2018, she was inducted into the YWCA Canton Women's Hall of Fame. An award-winning photographer, she has produced photo series such as *A Long Time Ago: The Fairytales of Mandy Altimus Pond* (2014); *Face of Hunger in Stark County* (2015); and a middle school student project, *Images of World War I* (2014). Stahl and her husband, Bryan, have one son, Donovan.

Appendix

Poland   1291 OFF & E.M   Germany

FROM OFLAG 64 TO STALAG XII B (HAMMELBERG) JAN 21 - MARCH 8. 1945

DATE	DISTANCE IN KM	TOWN	MISC.	DATE	DISTANCE KM	TOWN	MISC
JAN 21	21	(EXIN) Wogheim	Left 70	Feb 15	—	Rest	
22	26	Eichfield	OLEO	16	24	Murchin	
23	7	Charlottenberg	½ Bread . Oleo . cheese	17	27	Noenberg	
24	9	Lobsen	¼ Bread	18	—	Rest	1- Red Cross Parcel
25	16	Platow		19	11	Near Jarman	1/6 Bread
26	—	Rest	1 Loaf Bread 90 Left	20	21	Walkow	1/6 Bread
27	17	Jastrow	¼ Bread Oleo - 120 Left	21	—	Rest	½ Red Cross Pa
28	16	Zippnow		22	17	Noukalen	1/6 Bread
29	8	Oflag II B	100 Left	23	19	Basador	1/3 Bread
30	12	Marcheim	1-Loct Bread	24	23	Cramen malchin	
31	14	Templeberg		25	22	Planhogen	1/3 Bread
Feb 1	7	Heindrichdorf	Bread & Oleo	26	—	Rest (Crameri)	
2	18	(Falkenberg) Zushagen		27	17	Luby	
3	—	Rest		28	15	Siggelskow	½ Red Cross Parcel
4	17	Gienew		Mar 1	—	Rest	
5	20	Zeitlitch	½ Bread Left - 100	2	—	"	
6	21	Regenwalde	½ Bread	3	—	"	
7	20	Hebbin (Grieffenberg)		4	—	"	
8	19	Stuchow		5	—	"	¼ Red Cross Parcel
9	14	Streson		6	11	Parchim	½ Bread Oleo Entraine
10	16	Dievenow	1-Bread - Oleo	46	568		
11	16	Neuendorf	OLEO	7	150	Magdeburg - 0700	Train
12	25	Swingmunoe	Left - 21	8		Hammelberg -	"
13	7	Garz	OLEO	9	6	Stalag XII B	Wallree
14	15	Stolpe	Left - 100	48 days	724 K.m.		
250	361						

Major William P. Moon transcription of his notes about the forced march from Oflag 64, Szubin, Poland to Stalag 13B Hammelburg, Germany. Page 1.

Appendix

HAMMELBERG TO Mooseberg - MAR 28 - APR. 20

DATE	KM	TOWN	MISC.		
Mar. 28		Left Hammelberg 0800	Rail		
29 30		FORKEIM - NURNBERG	1/3 RC Par		
APR 4		Left NURNBERG - 1400	Walking		
		Spent night in woods			
5		Walked all day & night	REST		
6		marched 11 km Berching	1/2 RC Par		
7	20	Sandersdorf			
8		REST			
9	16	Newstadt	1/2 RC 1/2 Bread		
10	14	Neideremulsdorf	1/10 Bread		
11		REST			
12		"	1/9 Bread		
13	4	Morgensterleo			
14		Rest	2/5 Bread		
15		"	4/5 Bread potatoes		
16	12	Helshausen			
17		REST			
18	7	Schwarzendorf	1/4 RC Par		
19		Rest			
20	8	Mooseberg	1/3 Bread		
29		Liberated by 14 Armd Div 47 Inf Bn. 3d Army 99 Div			

Major William P. Moon transcription of his notes about the forced march from Stalag 13B Hammelburg, to liberation in Moosburg, Germany. Page 2.

Appendix
Additional Information

2 DEAD, 4 MISSING, 4 WOUNDED
Shell Fragment Kills Akronite In Foxhole

By HELEN WATERHOUSE

A SHELL SCREAMED over the Holland front.

Crouching in their foxholes a group of weary glider infantrymen raised their heads—breathed easy. It had passed safely over. But a little later one of them went to take cigarets to their comrade, P.F.C. James Kiss, in a nearby trench. What he saw made him turn back.

"I want to remember Jimmy as he was," he said. "A splinter of the shell must have struck him but I couldn't touch him—"

This was the tragic story as written home to Mrs. Joe Kiss, of 711 Harvard st., by a girl friend of the Akron soldier living in England. She had learned the details from one of the buddies in the other foxhole. But Mrs. Kiss still won't believe her son is gone. "Perhaps he was just badly hurt," she says in spite of a killed in action telegram from the government.

Kiss is one of two men reported killed in action. Four others were reported missing, and four wounded.

The casualties:

Killed
PVT. BERNARD BUEHLER, 27, of 1305 Coventry st., in Philippines.

P.F.C. JAMES S. KISS, 28, of 711 Harvard st., in Holland.

Missing
PVT. ROBERT J. LEONARD, 25, of 2621 Elmwood st., Cuyahoga Falls, in Germany.

P.F.C. WILLIAM A. ARNOLD, JR., 24, of 421 E. Buchtel av., in Belgium.

CAPT. JOHN J. MOHN, 25, of 718 Crosby st., in Germany.

LIEUT. ROBERT H. LIND, 24, of 815 Troy pl., Canton, in South American waters.

Wounded
P.F.C. JOHN H. MUSCH, 20, of 2483 Nesbitt av., in France.

STAFF SERGT. ALBERT J. HUMPHREY, 22, of 841 Keeney st., in Belgium.

LIEUT. GEORGE E. CLARKE, 28, of 1201 19th st., NW Canton, in France.

LIEUT. ROBERT F. MOHN, 24, of 316 Sumner st., in Italy.

ONE OF THE reasons why Mrs. Kiss will not believe her son died on Oct. 13, as the belated wire stated, is that she received 50 golden chrysanthemums from him on Christmas day—her 50th birthday.

Also a series of conflicting wires came to her before the final one announcing his death. All arrived within a week. The first said that the glider trooper was missing in action—the second told her he was safely back with his outfit and the third was the death wire. Kiss had previously been wounded in action when his glider ran into a tree on D-day.

Kiss was an only son. He had served overseas for a year, taking part in several glider invasions. He was formerly employed at the Acme store at Wallhaven.

PVT. BERNARD BUEHLER, killed in Philippines

P.F.C. JAMES S. KISS, killed in Holland

Leonard   Arnold

Capt. Mohn   Musch

Humphrey   Lieut. Mohn

VICTIM OF the Jap counter attack on Leyte, Private Buehler was killed Dec. 14 when most of the action at that island was apparently over, his mother believed.

Mrs. Lena Buehler had just received a letter from her son, written the very day he died, in which he spoke of building barracks on the island. He was also serving as assistant to the chaplain there, he said.

Buehler was an altar boy at St. Paul's Catholic church in Firestone Park before entering service. Memorial high mass will be sung for him at that church at 9:30 a. m. Tuesday.

Formerly employed at the Imperial Electric Co., Buehler had already seen plenty of action in the Pacific. He had been in combat at Attu and the Kwajalein atoll since going overseas two years ago. Besides his mother, Buehler leaves three brothers, Paul and Herbert of Akron and Ernest, of Cuyahoga Falls. He also leaves a sister, Mrs. Mary Kocsis of California.

* * *

JOHN A. MOHN, 256 Carroll st., is father of the two Mohn brothers. Captain Mohn has been missing in action in Germany since Dec. 16. His brother, Lieut. Mohn, was wounded in the Italian battlefront in the fall.

Captain Mohn is the husband of Catherine Mohn. He had been overseas only two months when lost.

Lieutenant Mohn, the wounded brother, is the husband of Helen Mohn. He is a graduate of West high school and attended Akron university. He had been serving for two years in the air corps when he was wounded.

* * *

MEMBER OF an anti-aircraft battalion, Private Arnold was lost in action in Belgium Dec. 20, his father, William H. Arnold, sr., has learned.

He had been overseas almost three years, having been sent to Iceland. He has served five years in the army.

Missing since Dec. 21 in Germany is Private Leonard, a Stow high school graduate. The missing soldier was a former well known football and basketball player while at school. He is the husband of Mrs. Ruth E. Leonard and has two children, Linda, 5, and Janet, 4.

Private Leonard is the son of Mrs. Sadie Leonard and has two

BEACON JOURNAL RATION CALENDAR

MEATS AND FATS
Book four red stamps Q-5 through X-5 good for 10 points each. None will be invalidated before March 1. Next series become valid Jan. 28.

CANNED GOODS
Book four blue stamps X-5, Y-5 and Z-5 and A-2 through G-2 new good for 10 points each. None will be invalidated before March 1. Next series become valid Feb 1

1945			JANUARY			1945
S	M	T	W	T	F	S
		1	2	3	4	5	6
7	8	9	10	11	12	13
14	15	16	17	18	19	20
21	22	23	24	25	26	27
28	29	30	31			

SUGAR
One sugar stamp 34 valid now for five pounds. Another will be validated Feb. 1. All canning sugar coupons invalid

SHOES
Stamps one, two and three on "airplane" sheet in book No. 3 good for one pair each indefinitely.

FUEL OIL
Old period four and five coupons good throughout current heating season. New period coupons one, two and three also valid and good through heating year.

LIQUOR
Two quarts, two fifths or four pints of whisky allowed on No 19 period expiring Jan. 27. All other liquors unrationed.

TIRES
Inspections not compulsory unless applying for tires. Commercial vehicle tire inspection every six months or every 1,000 miles whichever is first.

GASOLINE
Stamp A-14 in new book good for four gallons through March 21. B-5, B-4 and C-5 and C-6 good for five gallons until used. Non-highway gasoline stamps E-1 valid for one gallon each, stamps R-1 valid for five gallons each until used. Mileage record rationing record required in applying for supplemental gasoline rations

"Shell Fragment Kills Akronite In Foxhole," January 15, 1945
Reprinted with permission of the Akron Beacon Journal and Ohio.com.

Special Thanks

Ed McHugh for historic insights provided and his review of the publication.

Dr. Leslie Heaphy, Kent State University, Stark Campus for her encouragement of Mandy's film documentary about John Mohn's forced march.

Lois McHugh for her assistance with scanning images and yearbooks.

The Akron/Summit Library for their assistance in finding the newspaper article with John Mohn's P.O.W. information.

Keith Ward for granting permission to reprint several of his images in this book. (**https://www.flickr.com/photos/kawkawpa**)

Kim Anderson and Bruce Winges of the Akron Beacon Journal, Ohio.com for their assistance in granting the rights to reproduce that newspaper.

Sarah Zimmer at Getty Images for her licensing assistance.

Gunter G. Gillot Jr. of European Military Center for History, eucmh.com, for granting permission to reprint several images in this book.

Mike Bardin, formerly of the Ohio Society for Military History in Massillon for his display of John J. Mohn's military collection.

106th Infantry Division Association for recording the story of the brave 106th and keeping it alive all these years.

Sherie Brown and Jessica Watkins of Massillon Public Library for sponsoring the book launch for this publication. of the first edition on May 6, 2015.

Margy Vogt for her assistance with media releases.

Second Edition:

Glenn W. Russell for sharing "Roads To Liberation From Oflag 64" by Clarence R. Meltesen which provided corroboration for many stories in this book. His interest was prompted by the fact that his uncle, Capt. Charles Russell, neighbor, Lt. Robert McBrier, and his wife's family doctor, Maj. Charles Serbst, were POWs at Oflag XIII-B and all were captured at the Battle of Bulge.

Made in United States
Orlando, FL
11 June 2025

62013887R00077